D

THE
PREGNANCY
PROJECT

THE PREGNANCY PROJECT

A MEMOIR

Gaby Rodriguez
with Jenna Glatzer

SIMON & SCHUSTER BFYR

NEW YORK LONDON TORONTO SYDNEY NEW DELHI

SIMON & SCHUSTER BFYR

An imprint of Simon & Schuster Children's Publishing Division
1230 Avenue of the Americas, New York, New York 10020

For information about special discounts for bulk purchases, please contact Simon & Schuster
Special Sales at 1-866-506-1949 or business@simonandschuster.com.
The Simon & Schuster Speakers Bureau can bring authors to your live event. For more
information or to book an event, contact the Simon & Schuster Speakers Bureau at 1-866-248-
3049 or visit our website at www.simonspeakers.com.
Book design by Hilary Zarycky
The text for this book is set in Electra.
Manufactured in the United States of America
2 4 6 8 10 9 7 5 3 1
Library of Congress Cataloging-in-Publication Data
Rodriguez, Gaby.
The pregnancy project : a memoir / Gaby Rodriguez with Jenna Glatzer.
p. cm.
Summary: "The true story of a high school senior whose faked pregnancy rocked her community
and made international headlines. Growing up, Gaby Rodriguez was often told she would end up
a teen mom. After all, her mother and her older sisters had gotten pregnant as teenagers...from an
outsider's perspective, it was practically a family tradition. Gaby had ambitions that didn't include
teen motherhood. But she wondered: How would she be treated if she "lived down" to others'
expectations? Would everyone ignore the years she put into being a good student and see her as
just another pregnant teen statistic with no future? These questions sparked Gaby's school project:
faking her own pregnancy as a high school senior to see how her family, friends, and community
would react. What she learned changed her life forever, and made international headlines in the
process. In The Pregnancy Project, Gaby details how she was able to fake her own pregnancy—
hiding the truth from even her siblings and boyfriend's parents—and what it was like to become an
accidental overnight media sensation, trying to navigate a new world of film and book offers and
talk show invitations while getting ready for the prom. But more than that, Gaby's story is about
the power of stereotypes, and how one girl found the strength to come out from the shadow of low
expectations to forge a bright future for herself"— Provided by publisher.
ISBN 978-1-4424-4622-9 (hardback) — ISBN 978-1-4424-4624-3 (ebk)
1. Teenage pregnancy—United States. 2. Stereotypes (Social psychology) 3. Rodriguez, Gaby.
I. Glatzer, Jenna. II. Title.
LB3433.R63 2012
306.874'3—dc23
2011038862

FIRST EDITION

To my mother, Juana Rodriguez, who means everything to me. And to all the teen moms who didn't have the support they needed to follow their dreams, you're in my heart.

—G. R.

PART I
CONCEPTION

CHAPTER 1

BEFORE THERE WAS ME

For a moment, I understood just what it must be like to be a celebrity caught in the middle of a scandal. There I was, on a senior class field trip, *in disguise*, and running away from a reporter and cameraman who had followed me, trying to sneak a quote out of me for their story. That's because I'm The Girl Who Faked Her Own Pregnancy as a Senior Project. Okay, it's not an official title, but it might as well be. Overnight I went from being just another unknown seventeen-year-old girl in small-town Washington State to an international media sensation. It was weird.

Weird and scary.

I sure hadn't planned on any of it. When *Good Morning America* called my school looking for me while I was in the midst of juggling four other interviews, I ran out the back door crying. Who was I to be on national television? And it wasn't just *Good Morning America*—all the major television networks in the United States, plus some international ones, wanted to send film crews out to my little hometown to talk to me. Three of them came to my school to give presentations and try to woo me for my first "exclusive." And in addition to the news programs, there were also movie producers, talk-show hosts, radio producers, newspaper and magazine editors, book publishers. . . . My principal nearly went out of his mind trying to keep up with the calls that had resulted from my project.

They all wanted to ask the same questions: *Why did you do it? You really didn't tell your boyfriend's parents? What do you think of shows like* Teen Mom *and* 16 and Pregnant? *What's your message?*

I worried about saying the wrong things. I worried I would be misinterpreted or misquoted or just plain misunderstood. I didn't know how to turn my message into a sound bite for the media—how do you explain a lifetime in just a sentence or two?

Because that's what it was, really. This wasn't merely a senior project that I picked out of a hat, hoping for a good grade and the chance to go on *The Today Show*. It was something that reflected a major issue in my family, which started with my mom decades before I was born. And if you're going to understand my story, I first need to tell you about my family and where I grew up.

• • •

My mother is a superhero. I know this because I've seen her in action, under the hood of a car that is probably better suited for the junkyard than the highway. She learned how to fix cars by watching mechanic shows on television and by studying what other people did when they worked on their cars. That's how she figured out how to fix washing machines and other appliances around the house, too. Even when she was eight months pregnant with me, she was rolling herself underneath a car to fix something or other, because that's what needed to be done. Give her enough time and she can figure out nearly anything.

She didn't learn these skills in school—she dropped out when she became pregnant in the eighth grade, at age fourteen. I learned that when I was in about the seventh grade, and it seemed unreal to me. *I'm just a kid*, I thought. *How could she have had a baby when she was just one grade above me?*

I always knew my mother had been young when she had her first child, but I never did the math, never realized that she was in middle school. And when she first told me she had Nievitas at fifteen, I assumed that meant she got pregnant when she was fifteen. Then she corrected me and said she got pregnant when she was fourteen, and for some reason that pushed it over the edge for me. Fifteen was still a couple of years away, but fourteen was too close

5

for comfort. Some of my friends were fourteen. Picturing them with babies was crazy.

"I made a mistake," my mother said. "But Gaby, this is not a road I want you to go down. This is not an option for you. You have a good life ahead of you, and I want you to wait until you're ready before you have kids. Focus on school and think about relationships later."

I was listening, but also distracted by the implications of what she was telling me about her life. It's hard for me to even think about how she coped. In middle school, I was just starting to figure out who I was; I was thinking about my schoolwork and my friends and sports and what I might like to do with my future. My mother had to think about what time the baby had her last feeding, whether they had enough diapers in the house, and scheduling doctor visits for immunizations and check-ups. She didn't have her own life anymore. Motherhood swallowed her up.

The summer before I took sex ed class in middle school, my mom decided to tell me the whole story. We had looked over my upcoming curriculum together, and my mom had to sign off on a note saying that she acknowledged that I would be taking sex ed as part of my health and fitness class the following year. I wondered aloud what they would teach us. She figured they'd probably talk to us about abstinence and protecting yourself from unwanted pregnancy and sexually transmitted diseases, and that led into the first of our frank talks about her past. I'm not sure anymore whether she started the conversation or I did; whenever I had questions, she always respected me enough to answer honestly, but she tried to protect my feelings by not sharing some of the more difficult details until she felt I was ready to hear them.

Her father had died of cancer when she was eight years old, and she was the second-oldest in a family of eight kids. There would have been ten, but one of my grandmother's pregnancies ended in miscarriage, and another baby was premature and died in infancy. Three girls and five boys remained. After her father's death, her mother reared all the kids alone, and she was deeply disappointed when my mother got pregnant at such an early age. My mom cared very much what her mother thought, especially because that was the only parent she had left.

Because her mother wouldn't have it any other way, my mother explained, she married the boy who impregnated her. Secretly she hoped he would move back to Mexico so she'd be relieved of her duty to stay with him, but he stuck around and decided he liked the idea of having a wife to do the chores for him and be at his beck and call in the bedroom. Although she wanted to go back to school, he wouldn't let her. Instead, she went to work at a potato plant warehouse. He worked in the fields driving tractors and trucks, a job that usually went to illegal immigrants, though he was a citizen. They had seven children together over the course of their sixteen-year marriage—all my brothers and sisters, but not me. I wasn't born until years later.

Three girls and four boys. In birth order, they are: Nievitas, Genaro, Sonya, Javier, Fabian, Tony, and Jessica.

There were lots of physical fights between my mom and her husband, her husband and the kids, and between the kids themselves. One story my siblings told me that always stands out in my mind is about a fight that started when their dad was at work and my mother decided to run to the grocery store, leaving the older kids in charge of the younger kids. After all, the older ones were teenagers, and all the kids were just sitting in the living room watching television when she left. She figured she would be gone a short time, so what could go wrong?

Jessica, the youngest, was four or five at the time. She was sitting on the windowsill, watching the cars go by and waiting for Mom to come home. When she got up to go to the bathroom, she didn't want to lose her good spot, so she threatened Fabian: "If you're sitting in my spot when I get back, I'm going to get a gun and shoot you."

Guess he didn't take her at face value.

She came back and, sure enough, he was sitting in her spot. So she went off to her oldest brother's room, got his BB gun, pointed it at Fabian's face, and shot him in the eye.

My mother and their father came home at the same time and saw this horrible scene. My mother ran to Fabian to look at the damage, and their father took the BB gun and cracked it over Genaro's head.

He didn't want to blame Jessica—she was the baby of the family, after all—so he blamed Genaro for having the gun in the house to begin with. Beating on Genaro came before taking Fabian to the hospital. He's still partially blind in that eye to this day.

My mother is a gentle woman who was raised by a gentle woman, but the abuse didn't cause her to leave. Her husband was the only real boyfriend she'd ever had, considering she got pregnant at fourteen. She had such little life experience and relationship experience; she didn't know what was normal and acceptable, and she didn't feel like she had a choice. Her mother made her feel like she had to stick it out no matter what because she got pregnant. So for many years, she just accepted that this mistake was going to cost her the rest of her life.

I think that if she had waited until she was older to get married and have kids, she would have had a very different perspective. She would have been able to stand up for herself, and she would have had the confidence to know she could make it on her own if she needed to.

After sixteen years, the rumors started getting to her— word around the neighborhood was that her husband was being unfaithful to her. At first she brushed the gossip aside. What did these busybodies know, anyway?

But then there were little signs . . . his clothes in the laundry would smell of perfume that wasn't hers, or he'd come home later at night. When she saw him driving his work van past the house at a time when he was supposed to be elsewhere, she decided to follow him in the family station wagon . . . a bold move for a woman who had been taught to obey her man without question.

The car parked in an unfamiliar place: a local bar. My mother had never been in a bar in her life, and had no idea that her husband ever frequented them, either. He drank plenty, openly and in front of the kids, but she didn't know he went out to places like this. She walked into the dimly lit room, and there he was—with his arm around a woman, sharing a beer with her.

My mother approached him, her body stiff with shock.

"What are you doing here?" she asked him.

He looked up, dropped his hold on the other woman, and yelled, "You're *following me* now? What do you think you're doing? You go home right now, and don't you ever come following me again!"

All the bad names she could call him raced through her mind. Part of her wanted to scream at him, humiliate him, but she held back. She just stared at him, nodded, and left him there with that woman, whoever she was.

He's worth nothing, she thought.

But a short time later, he came home acting repentant,

got on his knees, and begged her forgiveness. He had just been shocked to see her there, he said, and he was sorry, and it wouldn't happen again. With seven kids to care for, she agreed to give him another chance.

Weeks later, he tried to commit suicide. He blamed it on her, saying that he had cheated because he thought *she* was cheating. They got into fights that involved the police. Then she contracted a sexually transmitted disease from him, and she decided she'd had enough. She'd put up with the drinking and the abuse and the way he treated her like his personal servant, but she drew the line at cheating. She told him she wanted a divorce.

They raced each other to the courthouse, with him speeding about a hundred miles per hour down the freeway while she tried to catch up. But he got there first and filled out the paperwork. He wanted to be sure that *he* was divorcing *her* and not the other way around. He also filed a petition for full custody of the kids and got a court order forcing her to leave the house—a trailer home they owned. He wouldn't let her take the kids with her, which she thought was just his way of punishing her.

She had no idea what he said or did to get the order that kept her out of the house. She moved back in with her mother and waited for the court date so a judge could straighten this out. It worried her to leave her kids with him alone, but every time she tried to see them, he'd call the police to have her thrown off the property.

What happened next is hard for her to talk about, and I don't press the issue much. You could certainly say she'd made her share of mistakes before, but this mistake would haunt her the rest of her life.

She couldn't afford an attorney, but she didn't think she'd need one anyway. There wasn't much to split or to talk about, as far as she figured it—but he figured differently. He hired a ruthless attorney and had his brother come talk to the judge about what an unfit mother she was. It stunned her that this brother would say such things about her when she had devoted her life to her family, but he twisted tales to make her sound neglectful. And her ex spun the story about how he kicked her out of the house and made her leave the kids behind into "She *abandoned* them."

Not only did the judge buy it, but he ordered my mother out of the house permanently, with nothing whatsoever except the clothes on her back. She was to leave immediately, with no money, no car, no possessions—and she would have to pay *him* child support because he would have custody of the kids.

From the courthouse, she had to drive the kids back to their father's home, and she cried most of the way. She didn't know how to explain to them what had gone wrong and why she had to leave them. Her visitation time was limited to three hours a week, on Mondays from six to nine p.m. Every time she tried to visit more than that, he said he would call the police.

To make matters worse, her ex's brother, who had testified against her in court, was married to my mother's sister. Although her sister wanted to be supportive, it wasn't possible for my mother to fully trust her again. She was on "the other team" now. On the other hand, several members of his family would still visit her or talk sweetly to her when they ran into her, telling her that they loved her and would rather have her in their family than him. They knew what his temper was like, and they didn't approve of the way he'd cheated on her.

Seasonally, she worked at Snokist, a fruit production warehouse that canned apples, pears, cherries, and prunes; the rest of the time, she got by on welfare checks. She felt completely lost and had no idea what steps to take.

Please, God, lift me up, she prayed. *This can't be my life.*

When a friend offered her a chance to tag along with him to Montana, she accepted. She wanted time away to clear her mind and figure out how to get on her feet again and get her kids back. After sixteen years of caring for others—her entire adult life, plus some—she had no idea how to care for herself. Her world had been very small, and she was naïve to the way the legal system worked. All she knew was that a judge had ruled that she couldn't see her kids.

It was around October, and there was black ice all over

the mountain roads as she drove the friend's car toward Montana. My mother had never had any kind of experience driving on ice. On a downhill slope, the car accelerated faster and faster, out of control, and slid from side to side. She jerked the wheel to try to regain control, but it had the opposite effect. In a terrifying second, the car hit the median and started rolling over onto the passenger side. Her scared friend tried to jump out of the car, but his head got caught and he slid on his face across the pavement. Most of the skin was ripped off his face, and he moaned in pain.

Don't die. Please, not like this, she thought.

She was trapped in the car, honking the horn and praying that someone would hear. Someone did. It turned out that there had already been five accidents on the road that day. Rescuers in a semitruck broke a window to reach her, then laid her down in the truck and started driving away.

"No, I can't leave! You have to get him out first!" she said, but they insisted on getting her to a hospital and promised they would get him help quickly. At the hospital, she found out her friend had died. Maybe the rescuers had realized that at the scene and were trying to spare her from finding out right away.

Now she was terrified to face her family, and the ex-husband who had just taken away their children. How was she going to live with herself? What would they say about her?

More lost than ever, she spoke to another friend, who asked her, "What do you want to do? Do you want to go back home or keep moving?"

"I want to move forward," she said. He was about to move to Kansas, where he had some family, and he offered to take her. My grandmother had lived in Kansas for a short period of time when she was younger, and had always told my mom that it was really pretty there. So my mom went with him and found work as a waitress in a restaurant. After several months, the friend told her he was in love with her and wanted to be her boyfriend. She was surprised, but accepted. They stayed together, and every couple of months she'd have enough money to go back and visit her kids. Each time, she tried to bring them back with her, but her ex would not allow her to.

Then one day came when she checked the mailbox and found a letter her boyfriend had written, addressed to someone in Mexico. He had forgotten to put a stamp on it, so the mail carrier hadn't taken it. My mother peeked—and found a letter professing his love to this Mexican woman who was apparently the mother of his children.

"When were you going to tell me about this?" she asked him. But he had no good answer. Realizing that she had nothing to stay for and that her life was in no better shape in Kansas than it had been almost a year earlier when she left Washington, she headed back.

Soon after my mother returned, the kids arrived home from school one day to find their mobile home missing and their belongings packed up and left on the property.

In a hurry, their father had sold the mobile home for $8,000—far less than it was worth—and decided he was moving to Walla Walla, Washington, with a new girlfriend. Walla Walla is known for its wine, sweet onions, and the largest penitentiary in the state of Washington.

My oldest brother, Genaro, was away in Job Corps, and my oldest sister, Nievitas, had left to live with her boyfriend in their former hometown, Warden, but the rest of them still lived with their dad at the time . . . yet he decided that the only child he wanted to take with him was the youngest, Jessica, who was probably six years old by then. He sent Fabian and Tony to live with their aunt in Oregon, then he handed my second-oldest sister, Sonya, about twenty dollars and told her to take care of her little brother Javier. They had no idea this was going to happen; the first time they realized that they were to be left behind was when they found their bags packed out by the curb that day and their home literally *missing*.

Why had he taken them away from the mother who wanted them if this was what he would turn around and do less than a year later?

Sonya and Javier had nowhere to go and no phone, so they walked to Nievitas's house. Luckily they knew the way.

My mom found out about all of this when Nievitas called her to say that she was watching over Sonya and Javier. At that point, the kids didn't really know how to feel about my mother—they'd been told she had left them behind. But Nievitas thought my mother should know what was happening and come get her children.

It had to be done in three stops. My mother first went to Nievitas's house and picked up Sonya and Javier, then headed to her ex-sister-in-law's house to get Fabian and Tony. The ex-sister-in-law readily gave them over to her. She still liked my mother very much and probably didn't want to be involved in this mess to begin with.

The most concerning part, though, was finding Jessica, who she felt would be the most vulnerable, especially because she was separated from her siblings. From the stories they've told me about their father, I can just say that it seems he drank a lot, fought a lot, and had volatile mood swings that worried all of them. The word they've used to describe him is "cruel." But at least until then, they had each other for protection from his anger.

My mother didn't really know where Walla Walla was, much less where Jessica might be in it, but miraculously, as she drove around the first corner in the town, she saw Jessica standing on the street. She was staying at a shelter with her father and his new girlfriend. My mother went to the courthouse and asked for paperwork to modify the custody orders.

She didn't want to go back to court, especially since it had gone so wrong for her the first time, but she prepared herself anyway. Thrusting the paperwork at her ex, she said, "I'm going to submit this to the court if you don't give her back to me right now."

Custody was never legally transferred to my mom because she never filed the papers. He gave Jessica up without a fight because he'd been having problems with Jessica's behavior. She was probably the most affected by their divorce. In her mind, then and even now, my mother had abandoned her.

Many of them still feel that way. There's a grudge that's sometimes spoken and sometimes unspoken, but it's always there. *She left us.* It mostly comes out when they're mad for other reasons. Sometimes that makes her cry. There's nothing she can do to change the past.

It was about a year, all in all, that she was away from them. Following that, except for the two oldest who were off on their own, my mom had her kids back. She tried to figure out a way to support the five of them, plus herself. Since custody wasn't legally hers, she didn't go after child support. They shared a four-bedroom house with her brother, sister-in-law, and their kids in Yakima, Washington. The kids doubled and tripled up in the bedrooms. My mom worked overnight shifts at three factories—and still managed to cook wonderful meals and do the shopping and care for the house and the kids.

Then my oldest sister, Nievitas, announced that she was pregnant.

My mother sank into depression; she didn't want history to repeat itself. At seventeen, Nievitas hadn't graduated from high school yet, and now she probably wouldn't. For a short time, her boyfriend stuck around. Then he was gone, and my mother had to pick up the slack. She thought she was done taking care of babies . . . but she wasn't—not by a long shot.

A year after Nievitas had her daughter, a bigger shock came along.

Me.

CHAPTER 2

WHERE MY STORY BEGINS

Twenty years after giving birth to her first child, my mother had me at age thirty-five, meaning that she became a grandmother before she became a new mother again. She never wanted to remarry and definitely wasn't planning to have any more kids—seven was quite enough—but she had been dating. This was now five years after her divorce, and the man she was with was a Mexican man whom she'd met while at a dance with friends. The second time she saw him was at another dance. He needed a ride home, so she offered to take him.

He wasn't so jealous or angry like her ex, but he was not daddy material, either. In fact, when my mother found out she was pregnant, he had already broken up with her. She didn't bother to track him down to tell him; she thought it

20

would be simpler for everyone involved if she just went on without him. There's no father listed on my birth certificate.

So you can imagine her surprise when she saw him a year and a half after their breakup at the local unemployment office, and his first words to her were "I know you had my child."

"I don't know what you're talking about," she said.

"You do. I know I have a daughter, and I want to know where she is."

She never found out how he knew—or, considering that he did know, why he never came asking about her before. We still lived in the same house in Yakima, so it's not as if we were in hiding.

She finally acknowledged the truth, and he said, "I want to be in her life. In both of your lives."

The first time he saw me was when I was ten months old, shortly after they ran into each other.

My mother had mixed feelings about it because she didn't want me to be hurt. She thought that no father at all would be better than an unreliable one, but I'm glad that I do at least know who my father is. Every child should have at least that much.

After that, my father would come around for a few months or a year at a time, then disappear for just as long, only to reappear unexpectedly. He never made a commitment to her or to me.

Having an absent father, like I did most of the time, can lead to all sorts of problems. There have been so many studies about the effects the lack of a father has on kids. Some are things you'd probably expect: Kids who don't have dads in their lives are more likely to be depressed, have behavioral problems, and drop out of school. But one of the other common effects is that girls who don't have dads around start having sex earlier and are more likely to be teen mothers. Girls without dads sometimes look for male attention and affection wherever they can find it, which isn't a healthy way to go about life.

A big study at the University of Canterbury found another intriguing aspect of that effect, too: Girls with stepfathers were likely to start having sex even younger than girls with no fathers in their lives at all. The researchers suggested that maybe it was because the girls were mimicking their mothers' dating habits. Or maybe it was because the stepfather was really in the family because of the mother, and the girl wanted to find a man who'd pay attention just to her.

I knew that my mother and father weren't together like the couples I saw on television. I picked up on the fact that my mom didn't go out on dates with my dad, and didn't hug and kiss him, and didn't talk to him except when it involved me. I wished they were married, mostly just because he was my dad and I wanted him around more. I think all kids want to see their parents together.

My dad was an immigrant who worked in the fields. Shortly after he found out about me, he got married and had a child with his new wife. His oldest daughter is three years younger than I am. My mother kept letting him come back into my life whenever he showed up, even though she knew it wouldn't last and even though he paid no child support when he vanished. She once filed for court-ordered child support, but the agency informed her that they were unable to find him, so they dropped her petition.

She'd never before tried to raise a baby alone; her kids were five and up when she and her ex-husband split up. Doing the middle-of-the-night feedings and round-the-clock care a baby requires by herself was a much bigger challenge.

I'm the only one of my siblings with a different father, but they never made me feel different because of that. If anything, because they're so much older than I am, they seemed to take a stake in my well-being. A new baby is always a symbol of hope, an unblemished life with all the possibility in the world ahead of it.

From what I hear, I was a good baby. Happy, quiet. There are lots of pictures of my brothers holding me or sitting with me on their laps on the couch. They liked helping my mom take care of me. I was yet another body to squish into that four-bedroom home, so once I was out of my crib, I slept in the same bed as my mom.

When I was about four, my dad made a necklace for

me; it was a cross that he wove with string, and it had three beads across the middle and one on top. There was no clasp, so I couldn't take it on and off. He tied it around my neck and I wore that thing every day, in the shower, in the pool, everywhere. You can see it in my kindergarten school photo. Wearing it made me feel like we were connected, like my dad was with me even when I had no idea where he was. I didn't question his whereabouts then, either . . . my mom figured she'd explain it to me when I asked, but I never did. I just accepted it as normal that a father would appear and disappear at will.

Somewhere along the line, the string on my cross started fraying and coming apart, so I took it off. My mom put it into a little pouch for me, along with a small photo of my dad. I still have it. The photo has turned yellow and brown with age.

We used to go together to the "Duck Park"—a local park that had a big pond in the middle of it where we could toss bread to the ducks and geese and walk around. We never remembered the real name of the park, so my dad just called it the Duck Park. My mom would drive there with me and I'd talk with him. I don't remember much about the conversations anymore, but my mom tells me that the visits were brief.

Sometimes we'd also go visit him at his apartment, which he shared with his brothers. They'd all go back and forth to Mexico and move around a lot depending on where they could find work.

24

My mom was still the center of my world. She did what she had to do without complaining, and I remember a lot of laughter and love no matter where we were.

I felt like my mom saw a possibility in me that had not yet been realized by the others in my family. I wanted to live up to her expectations.

Whenever she could, she bought me jigsaw puzzles, my favorite toy. As I got older, I loved doing more and more complex puzzles. Usually when someone completes a big puzzle, they'll glue the back of it and maybe hang it up because it was so hard to finish. Me, I loved finishing a puzzle only to tear it apart again and start over.

So, okay, I wasn't the *coolest* kid. In fact, I didn't have many friends because I was more comfortable keeping to myself and my family. My mother worked nights as far back as I can remember, and her shifts would often end after seven in the morning, which was when I needed to be in school. So on those days we'd sleep at my grandmother's house, where she lived with my uncle Felipe.

Felipe was diagnosed with schizophrenia at about age eleven, and takes multiple medications for it. When he doesn't take his medication on time, he gets very antsy and loses his perspective on reality versus fantasy. He watches something on television and believes it happened to him— and then will make up an elaborate story about how it happened. He can also get angry quickly.

He's not completely out of touch; he knows the date and who's president, for instance. On the other hand, he's never worked a day in his life and yet when my brothers come over and ask how he's doing, he'll say, "I've been working for eight years at this job and they don't pay me enough." He generally says his job is at the local tire center.

One of his odd habits is to wear jackets and multiple layers of clothing, even on the hottest days of summer. He would wear two or three jackets over his clothing if no one watched him, which made us worry that he could die of heatstroke. So my mom would have to hide his jackets and spot-check his layers of clothing—he'd change multiple times per day.

Felipe never really scared me, though I know some of my little nieces and nephews were uncomfortable around him. He would rant about things that didn't make sense, and his mannerisms were strange. But he mostly kept to himself.

When I stayed at their house, my grandmother would wake me and help me get ready. I didn't need to eat breakfast or pack a lunch because I could eat in school, so I'd just get dressed and walk there myself. After classes, I'd usually go over to the school library.

I loved reading all sorts of books. Still do. I could get lost in other people's stories and no one would bother me. And just like with the puzzles, when I found a book I really loved, I'd read it again and again.

There was a nice librarian named Ms. Carney who

taught me how to use computers, and that fascinated me. Once I went into middle school, I tried to pay back the favor by volunteering as a tutor to help the elementary school kids learn to read. It was good practice for me socially. This helped me expand my boundaries to kids who weren't directly related to me.

Both of my career goals at this point came directly from that library. I told my mom I wanted to be a teacher, mostly because I liked how it felt to teach those kids to read. But when it came time to discuss my career interests in middle school, I said that I wanted to go into computer science. My inquisitiveness and obedience made me a very good student, which made my mother proud.

Some of the possibilities for her other kids had been extinguished too soon because of their sexual behaviors, repeating the cycle that started with my mom. Soon after Nievitas's daughter was born, there would be more grand-kids out of wedlock. My brother Javier got his girlfriend pregnant at seventeen, then had two children with another girlfriend before meeting and marrying his wife. His oldest daughter lives in the same town we do, so he sees her often, but his other two daughters live out of state, and most of their contact is online and by phone. I know he sees them when he can and would like to see them more.

Fabian wasn't a teenage dad, but he was in his early twenties and not yet settled. He had dropped out of school and hadn't learned to hold down a job. He's still grappling with the idea of going back to get his GED now, because he's realized that education matters. He has four boys, and an ex-girlfriend who threatened to keep the kids away from him if he didn't stop chain-smoking. (He was up to three or four packs a day at one point, but he has at least cut down.)

My youngest brother, Tony, got his girlfriend pregnant when they were in high school. They're still together today, though, and have four children.

My second-oldest sister, Sonya, also dropped out of high school, got her GED, and married when she was nineteen. Two weeks after the wedding, she found out she was pregnant.

And then there was Jessica, the sister who's closest in age to me. When she was sixteen, she ran off to Mexico with her boyfriend and returned with a baby bump, alone. The boyfriend said he was going to come back for them, so she waited at home . . . and never saw him again.

I either wasn't born yet or wasn't old enough to remember any of the other pregnancies that came before hers, but I remember all my brothers and sisters being mad at Jessica. No one was talking to her except me; I didn't have any reason to be mad. I tried putting the pieces together to figure out why they were so upset. It was the first time I was old enough to understand that something could be wrong with pregnancy. I was eight then, so Jessica still seemed much older to me — I didn't connect their anger with her age. I just knew that they were mad she was pregnant, and mad she had run off to Mexico in the first place.

By that time, I already knew what sex was. As far as I recall, no one ever sat me down and had the classic "birds and bees" talk with me, but I figured it out anyway. Naïveté was a luxury I did not have as a child; there was too much reality all around me to stay in the dark about relationships. I knew that a woman had to have sex with a man in order to get pregnant, so I realized that Jessica had sex with her boyfriend in Mexico. I just wasn't sure why that might be a bad thing.

"When I find that guy, I'm going to beat him up," Javier would say.

They'd all agree, and then they'd grumble about how stupid Jessica was and how they all wanted to knock some sense into her.

"But what's the point? It's too late — she's already pregnant. Nothing we can do about it now," Genaro would say.

It's hard to understand why they didn't learn from each other; I guess they all needed to make their own mistakes. They have great kids, but it's never easy to have children before you're even fully grown yourself. There are the obvious financial problems, but there are also social problems — people will judge you differently, you can't just go out partying with your friends when you feel like it anymore, and people your age who don't have kids aren't going to understand what your life is like. Then there are problems with childcare—who's going to watch the kids when you work or go to school? And where's that money for daycare or babysitters going to come from? Around here, there are a lot of minimum-wage-type jobs that don't pay much more than daycare costs, so why bother?

So teenage parents depend on government assistance and never get back to that place where their lives are still open and full of possibilities. Eighty percent of them wind up on welfare. They can't figure out what they want to be when they grow up because they're too busy dealing with the responsibilities they created when they brought a child into the world. They don't get to think about becoming grown-ups; they just have to *be* grown-ups. It's a lot to give up for a night of sex.

Because they were dealing with their own families and their own problems now, my siblings weren't able to help my mom much while I was growing up in those early years, and my grandmother was the only close relative nearby. We lived at her house with Uncle Felipe on and off, and sometimes we just spent nights there to help my grandmother—as she got older, she needed more care. My mom was working, so this meant I was the one who got up in the middle of the night to check on my grandmother. Maybe it was this that made me feel older than my peers, more mature. I wasn't sure how to relate to them.

Starting when Jessica's baby was ten months old, I also babysat for him overnight when she wanted to go out partying with her friends on weekends.

I was maybe nine years old. She didn't want to live with us, so she moved in with our sister Sonya . . . who happened to live right next door. Sonya was already married, with kids of her own, and she was much more outspoken than I was. She would tell Jessica straight out, "I'm not watching your baby unless you pay me." Which meant that Jessica would walk next door and find me, and by the time she showed up, I was usually getting ready for bed.

"Mom's working, so you're going to have to take care of Carlos while I go out. Come here and I'll show you how to mix his formula."

She would point out the diapers, wipes, and bottles and then just go. She never asked; it was an order, something that was expected of me. Whenever she wanted to go out late at night, I would have to sleep next to the baby's crib, get up with him whenever he cried, change his diapers, feed him, dress him, rock him back to sleep, whatever he needed. I loved my nephew, but I did not want this job.

Even though he was not a "bad" baby, he was still a baby. Babies cry. They need things. They can't do anything for themselves, and they have no sense of timing. It left me feeling exhausted and run-down. I wasn't very good at standing up to any of my siblings; I would tell Jessica that I didn't want to do it, sometimes even very strongly, but I couldn't ever just say no. When she left, it was either me or nobody.

And what if something happened to the baby? My grandmother no longer drove, and I obviously couldn't, either, so if he got sick in the middle of the night or needed something, we would be stuck. I reasoned this through with her, but she just told me not to worry about it.

That's when I understood better why my brothers and sisters had been so mad, because now I was mad, too.

She shouldn't have gotten pregnant if she didn't want a baby, I thought.

The fact that Jessica was leaving the baby with me didn't sit well with my mom, who would often get into arguments with her about it.

"This is your responsibility, not Gaby's! She's just a child. You had this baby, and now it's time to grow up and act like a mother. You can't keep leaving Carlos with her. You have to stop going out and partying. That part of your life is over."

But she'd do it again anyway, and I'd again tell my mom, "I don't want to babysit anymore. This isn't fair." Then she'd go back to Jessica and yell at her again. I guess my mom eventually wore her out, and after she got a new boyfriend, Jessica stopped going out late at night with her friends. Soon thereafter, she was pregnant again. With twins.

"You're not married. You're not settled down with this

guy, but you still got pregnant again?" I asked her. I was about eleven then.

"Leave me alone. You don't know anything," she said.

It became clear to me that this was not a road I wanted to go down. I decided then and there that I was going to wait until I was married and had my own life in order before I brought a new life into the world. But my sisters and brothers didn't usually share this view. They continued having babies—second and third ones—and still didn't have their acts together. All in all, I have thirty-one nieces and nephews.

I wound up babysitting for almost all of the ones who are younger than I am, sometimes because my mother was working and other times because she had to sleep during the day when she came home from work. I was around and I worked for free, which was about all that qualified me. I babysat when my brothers or sisters needed to go to work or run errands, and I resented it. I was supposed to be out playing, and instead I was stuck watching all these kids. My patience quickly wore thin and I decided I didn't want to be a teacher after all, or a babysitter. Maybe I never wanted to see another kid again as long as I lived. The only thing that got me through was knowing that, in a few hours, I could hand them back to their mothers or fathers.

I didn't have that magic touch with babies like my mother had. She could hear a baby cry from across the room and diagnose exactly what was wrong.

"She has a bellyache," my mom would declare.

"How do you know?" one of my sisters would ask.

"I can hear the way she cries."

I guess raising eight babies of her own and several grand-kids made her a bona fide expert on baby cries. She could decipher whether a particular cry was from hunger, sleepiness, discomfort, or pain, and she knew just how to soothe babies. I, on the other hand, felt like I was starring in my own chapter of *Babies Are from Mars, Gaby Is from Venus*. I didn't have enough life experience to understand how to care for a child, nor did I want to. I just wanted to be a kid. And I didn't know how to do that particularly well, either.

I was not one of those kids playing Freeze Tag in the streets with the neighbors. Knowing how to talk to people didn't come easily to me, not like it did for some of my siblings. They were more outgoing and tried prodding me to come out of my shell. The lesson sank in sometime during my middle school years, when I made more of a concerted effort to be friendly. Javier had taught me that it was important to talk to all kinds of people, because you never knew when someone would be able to help you down the line, or when you'd be able to help them. He got the idea of community—and until then, I didn't. I saw only my own world.

He was the one who kept drumming into my head that I had to break the cycle for my family and do something to make my mother proud. Fifteen years older than me, he had been the "smart one," the one who had the biggest ambitions. But becoming a teen dad had significantly slowed down his track and made it much harder to get to where he wanted in life. It wasn't like he could just spend his time in college, studying and figuring out what he wanted to do. He had a family to support, which meant that he had to take whatever jobs he could find straight out of high school.

It's only now, at thirty-four years old, that he's getting to where he wants to be in life. He works as a companion home provider and counselor for developmentally disabled people and is interested in opening up his own group home.

Other kids might not have liked the pressure that Javier put on me, but I found it motivating. I did want to make my mother proud, after all. So I told myself that whatever paths presented themselves to me in life, I would always try to take the good ones.

CHAPTER 3

LIFE IN TOPPENISH

It took me a long time to realize that other people in my community didn't have any money, like us. I knew that we couldn't afford the things I saw on television and that our house looked nothing like the ones on sitcoms and in magazines, but it didn't occur to me that the whole town lived more like *we* did than like *they* did on TV. It was comforting to know we weren't the strange ones—but also sad to start thinking about how little opportunity there was here.

We moved from an average-sized house in Yakima to a very small house about twenty miles away in Toppenish, Washington, when I was five years old. We like to say it has three bedrooms, but that's probably pushing the definition of a bedroom. A real estate agent would say the house "needs TLC." My brothers have tried to help us when they could, but there are a lot of half-finished jobs in the house — like when my brothers fixed the roof but didn't put in any insulation, so our house stays very cold in the winter.

When we moved, I had to leave my dog behind. Muñeca, which is Spanish for "doll," was my big, brown, poufy Chow Chow. My grandmother was allergic to pet hair, and we were going to stay with her when we first arrived, which meant the dog couldn't come along. One of my brothers gave her to a friend of his. It was hard to let her go — she was a fun dog and part of my childhood that I didn't want to get rid of. Plus, I didn't think I was going to have any friends in Toppenish, and it would be lonely without her.

There are about 9,000 people in the city of Toppenish, which is on Indian reservation land. The slogan here is "Where the West still lives in the city of murals and museums." A little unwieldy, but that's what it is. So there are 73 historically accurate murals of Old West scenes and people, showing things like harvesting potatoes, clearing the land for farming, and playing the "Indian stick game." These beautiful murals are painted on walls and local business buildings — you'll find murals on the sides of dry cleaners and discount stores. Some walls were erected just to have murals painted on them. In the spring and summer, tourists can take a horse-drawn wagon ride to tour all the murals in town.

There's even a Toppenish Mural Society that sponsors a "Mural in a Day" every June, where twelve to fifteen artists are selected to paint a new mural together. Last year they redid a mural that was lost because the building it was on had to be knocked down.

Then there are the museums. First is the American Hop Museum, which bills itself as "the nation's only hop museum dedicated to showcasing the history of the obscure perennial vine bearing the botanical name *Humulus lupulus*." In other words, they display different types of hops used to make beer, along with the tools and equipment associated with the beer-making process. Then there's the Northern Pacific Railway Museum and the Yakama Nation Cultural Heritage Center.

Aside from the murals and museums, the other main attraction here is the Yakama Nation Legends Casino, where locals can get hired as line cooks or waiters if they're from the right tribe. Especially in the summer it's a tourist attraction, but year-round a lot of the locals go to the casino, too. That's not always a good thing, considering our community's economic status. My mom's friend once blew his whole tax refund in one day at the casino, and some of my friends' parents have real gambling problems. You can't gamble if you're under eighteen, but I've been there a handful of times to go to the buffet.

And while all that may sound really exciting (or, um, not), there's just not much else to do around here if you're a kid or teenager. There is a movie theater, but it doesn't show new releases. It shows movies after they've already been out for a couple of months, in that time between when they're in other theaters and when they come out on DVD. You can get tickets for three dollars, but most people don't want to wait that long to see a new movie, so they go to the next town and pay the eight or nine dollars instead.

The population here is more than 75 percent Latino or Hispanic. Within my school district, nearly 98 percent of students qualify for free or reduced-price lunches, a third of the students are still learning English, and a large percentage are from migrant families. About one of every five high school students here drop out of school and never come back to graduate, with pregnancy as one of the leading reasons.

Most teens get jobs (or at least try to) at places like McDonald's, Taco Bell, Dairy Queen, and Safeway. Some of them do it to have extra spending money for themselves, but a lot of them do it to kick in on the family bills. After all, our parents are also working at these same places, or on farms, or in the warehouses. Just about all of my friends have parents who work migrant jobs, and that means that none of us are living much over the poverty line.

When I began realizing that my family was really the norm around this city rather than the exception, it made me sad. We struggled too much, all of us, and it shouldn't be this way.

It shouldn't be this way.

As soon as I became aware of that, around age ten, I

made it a goal to leave Toppenish—not because I hated the town or the people in it, but because there just isn't much opportunity here. I had bigger dreams for myself. Nothing grandiose; I just wanted to have a job where I could make a real difference in people's lives, and make a comfortable living. And I didn't want my mom to have to fix her own beat-up cars anymore.

Throughout my life, my mother has been the constant. I can feel her love and support in everything I do. It has always been important to me to be a good student, both for my sake and for hers—I know she's very proud of my achievements in school. She's always wanted to go back and get her GED but has never been able to make the time. So in some ways, I'm helping her live out her own dreams, too. Whatever I achieve is because she has helped to lift me up and get me there, even when it's been at her own expense.

My mom is the kind of woman who always does for others first. There have been times when she owned just one pair of shoes, wearing them for everything from work to gardening, trying her best to keep them clean out in the dirt. As a kid, I didn't get why she honored so many of my sister Jessica's requests for new clothes and shoes while it was obvious my mom was struggling just for our basic needs. "You don't understand," my mom would explain quietly. "She's in high school. It's different for her."

She was right. I didn't understand what it was about high

school that made new sneakers important. Did the kids beat you up if you wore sneakers that were six months old? Maybe it wasn't really about that; maybe my mom was still compensating for the guilt she felt over the year she lost her kids. She kept trying to show them that she would do anything she could for them, to show that she hadn't left back then because she didn't care.

From the time I was born, on the other hand, my mom and I were inseparable. Aside from a vacation I'd taken with my oldest sister the previous year, the first time I really had to be apart from her was when I was twelve and she was going into the hospital. That's also the first time I can remember being terrified.

That year hadn't started well for our family. In January 2006, my grandmother got pneumonia, and we moved in with her to take care of her. It was easier for us to move to her house than to get her to us; she'd lived in the same house for forty-five years and was comfortable there.

When my mother worked, it was my job to watch out for my grandmother, which meant that I rarely got to sleep through the night. It wasn't an appropriate duty to give a child, but that's what happens when you're a single mom — there was no husband to help my mom, so she had to rely on me. She just didn't have a choice.

My grandmother wore an oxygen machine, and I wasn't able to sleep deeply because I kept worrying about the machine. What if it failed? What if she rolled over and accidentally unplugged it? Every couple of hours, I'd involuntarily wake up and find myself going to the living room to watch my grandmother breathe and make sure the machine was functioning correctly. I always made it on time to school the next day.

My grandmother also needed help getting up and walking around or she was likely to fall. Felipe would help her up and steady her when we weren't there. It fell on us to take care of them because no one else would. Even though my mother had six other siblings besides Felipe, most of them lived far away.

Lupe and Remigio, my grandmother's sons in Texas, had once told her they would take the train someday to come see her. My grandmother's house was just a block away from the railroad tracks, and as she lost her memory, she would stare out the window and wait for their train to arrive. "Here come my sons," she would tell us. "Any day now, they're going to be here. They're coming on the next train." I didn't have the heart to correct her.

By the end of February, we had moved back into our house, though my mother went over to check on my grandmother and Uncle Felipe as often as possible. Then in March, she decided it was time to see a doctor. She had a lot of blood clots, and her abdomen had swollen as if she were pregnant again . . . which she definitely was not this time.

"I don't know what's wrong with me, but I need to find out," she told me.

After an ultrasound, she found out she had a cyst near her uterus that was the size of a melon. Doctors told her it was probably not cancerous, but it needed to be removed for lots of other reasons. For one thing, if it ruptured on its own, it could spread infection throughout her body and cause her tremendous pain. But I kept worrying that once they got a look at it, they were going to tell her it was cancerous.

I sure didn't trust hospitals. I probably saw too many scary things on television. People could go into the hospital for some silly little procedure, like to splint a broken pinkie finger or something, and pick up an infection and die three days later. She seemed calm about it, though. Probably, she was just trying to look calm so she could comfort me.

My mom believed in me, and I believed in her. And no matter what the world threw at us, we could get through it together. My life was not going to work without my mother. I had trouble concentrating in the days leading up to her surgery, and I spent a lot of time pleading with God in my mind.

"Mom, I'm so afraid you won't come back from the hospital."

"Don't worry. God knows you're too young to be without your mama. He wouldn't take me away from you."

I wanted to trust that she was right, but I just wasn't sure. So I made a bargain with God.

You can take my house away from me, or any of my stuff, but you can't take my mom.

We had a family barbecue the night before at Fabian's house, and my mom left early to prepare for the surgery. It was a good thing, too, because things got ugly that night. Genaro had been drinking too much and started a fight with Fabian, then left angrily.

Genaro had a baby who was only twenty-eight days old at the time, Elisandra Gabriella. Her middle name was named after me. She was his third daughter, his second with his current girlfriend. The baby was a perfect little vision, and so tiny. I'd held her head in the palm of my hand, and her legs stretched only far enough so her feet barely touched the inside of my elbow. I could hold her like that. She looked like an angel.

For reasons I will never understand, after Genaro had gone to sleep the night of the barbecue, his girlfriend fed and changed the baby and put her down to sleep in bed next to him, even though she knew he'd been drinking. When he awoke the next morning, he turned over and saw blood coming from his baby daughter's nose and mouth. She was unresponsive. He picked her up and ran to the living room, laid her on the floor and attempted CPR, then took her to the hospital, where she was declared brain dead.

"She'll be on life-support machines for the rest of her life," the doctor told him. "There is no chance she'll come out of this."

My brother had to make the decision to pull the plug on his baby daughter. She died within a few hours.

That same day, my mother had her surgery. Thank goodness it really was a benign cyst like the doctor had said. As soon as my mom was released from the hospital, she went straight to Elisandra's wake. Elisandra wore a white and peach dress, and death had not stolen her angelic appearance. She had been cleaned up and looked like she was just sleeping peacefully there, fragile and beautiful.

Genaro and his girlfriend didn't split up solely as a result of the baby's death, but they did end things a few months later. So now he had one daughter he rarely got to see who lived in Portland with her mother, and another who would have to go through the back-and-forth nature of a broken home.

It should have been enough tragedy, but the year was not done with our family yet. My cousin, who was also pregnant as a teen, slipped down a flight of stairs and landed on her bottom. When she landed, the placenta tore away from the baby. Although doctors immediately tried to deliver the baby, she was too premature and died sixteen hours later. There was another tiny casket.

Bad news is supposed to come in threes. Why did we get an extra?

It was the kind of year you can't wait to get through, the kind that leaves a scar on your memory. I was twelve then, just starting to come out of my shell. There was so much sadness in my family at the time, and it was hard sometimes to feel the weight of all that grief. I had two best friends: my mom and school. Although I prayed fervently for some relief, going to church didn't help take my mind off anything. Our church was such a calm and serious place that all I could do was focus inward on my own thoughts—which were usually sad thoughts about the hardships my family was going through.

I hadn't learned to open up to kids my own age, who often seemed immature to me, but I finally reached the point where I wanted to have friends. There had to be someone outside my family who I could talk to when things *inside* my family got this tough.

My first friends became the ones I got to know by default: the honors students.

The honors students tended to stick together; as long as we did well, we all continued to be in the same classes throughout high school. But we also had nonacademic classes with the other students, and once I'd built up my confidence a bit, I learned to make eye contact and at least introduce myself to them.

One of the nice things about my school was that there weren't really cliques. For the most part, it wasn't like in teen movies where the jocks pick on the nerds and the older kids torment the younger ones. I wasn't made to feel out of place because I was an honors student. I became friends with a boy I met in the library and made several more friends I'd sit with in the cafeteria.

I rarely had kids come to my house because it was so tiny and awkward. I still shared a bedroom with my mother, so on the rare occasions when friends would come over, we couldn't really play in "my" room, because my mother would be walking in and out or sleeping after a work shift. When I started visiting other friends' houses, I noticed the difference. For the most part, their houses were a lot bigger than mine, and they had their own rooms. We could sit on their beds and talk and play. Compared with the rest of the world, they still didn't have much financially—but compared with me, they had a lot.

My mother regularly babysat my nieces and nephews so my sisters could work. My normal routine after school was to come home and see if she needed any help. If not, I would spend some time with friends before returning to eat dinner and do homework. When the weather was warm, we'd meet up at the community pool just a couple of blocks from my house.

But no matter how wonderful my friends were, it always came back to my mom for me: She was the one who talked to me about everything that needed to be talked about. She was the one I sought out when I needed advice or comfort, or just to laugh together. When she hurt, so did I, and vice versa. I knew how much she had gone through just to get to this point and keep us afloat, and I wanted her efforts to be worth it. Whatever I did in life, I knew I wanted to make my mom proud.

Some of my favorite memories growing up were of the simplest things. When she wasn't working, she'd sometimes pick me up from school and we'd walk to the ice cream shop. She'd buy me an ice cream cone and we'd just talk. There weren't any secrets between us; she encouraged me to be open with her about my life the way she was open with me. She never tried to hide her mistakes; she figured that the best way to guide me was to keep communication open. It worked. I realized early on that, even though I loved all of them, I didn't want to follow in the footsteps of my family members. When my mother told me that education was the key to a better life, I listened. When she told me that I could do anything I wanted to, I listened. It seemed simple: Live a good life, have a good life. Why was it so difficult for people to get this?

I left 2006 behind feeling like the best thing I could do was to throw myself into my schoolwork and sign up for as many extracurricular activities as I could. I needed an escape, and school provided it for me. It was a place where I was too busy to get lost in my own sadness, and a place to pursue the possibility—the small possibility—that I could get out of Toppenish and earn a completely different life.

CHAPTER 4

QUINCEAÑERA

As I transitioned from middle school to high school, my dreams got a little clearer. Computer science might have been interesting, but it wasn't where I could make a difference in the world. The more I looked around me, at my family and my community, the more I knew I wanted to help. Everyone needs one person in their lives who believes in them. I've always had my mother, and I know how lucky I am. Not everyone has a mother who loves them and is there for them. Some kids even go through the ultimate abandonment—they end up in foster care their entire childhoods, bouncing from one family to another until they finally just age out of the system.

That's what happened to Dave Pelzer, author of the famous book *A Child Called "It."* I read it that year and it changed my life. His is a story of unthinkable abuse—his mother tortured him in twisted ways, like making him sit on a stove, drink ammonia, eat the contents of a diaper . . . She told him that he wasn't even a person, just an "It." In the book, Pelzer goes through his childhood with no support or help whatsoever—his alcoholic father doesn't do anything to intervene—until finally a teacher notices and begins the process of having him taken out of his mother's custody. That teacher may have saved his life, or his sanity. That's really all it takes: one person to notice, and care, and do the right thing.

Maybe that's where I can make a difference, I thought. *I could be that one person.*

I wanted to understand how a woman could get pregnant, go through those nine months, give birth, and then give up her child, or lose the child because of bad life decisions. Why would this happen? And what can we do as a society to stop this from happening? What was the difference among women who had abortions; women who abandoned, neglected, or abused their kids; and women who waited until they were ready and loved their kids?

I didn't have any of the answers yet, but I was determined to try to figure it out. Maybe, as my brothers and sisters kept telling me, I was just too young and inexperienced to understand these "grown-up" things. But according to our culture, I was not going to be too young for long. At fourteen, I was about to become a woman.

A quinceañera is a major rite of passage for Latina girls. It's a celebration for a girl who turns fifteen, and it's filled with more rituals and symbolic meaning than a sweet sixteen in other cultures is. It starts with a blessing in church, then there's a reception and a dance party. The parties take a long time to plan and can be as involved and expensive as weddings. For a couple of years, my boyfriend and I went to one every weekend, sometimes even two or three per weekend. Some were friends, and lots were friends of friends, where someone would invite us to tag along. We had to buy gifts only for close friends, thank goodness, or I don't know how we would have afforded it.

I started planning my celebration a year in advance. When I called my dad to tell him about it, I hadn't seen him since my eighth birthday, when he dropped off a cake and left. He said he would come to my quinceañera—but then again, he'd said a lot of things through the years that didn't happen. "I have my family and my job," he would explain. He was married with three other kids by then. He wasn't mean to me; he just wasn't there after those first few years, aside from occasional phone conversations.

I didn't ask any of the hard questions until I was thirteen. That's when I wanted to know why my dad wasn't around, why he didn't live with us like other dads lived with their kids.

"It's not because of you," my mom said. "He didn't even

know you were going to be born when we split up. We tried and tried to make it work, but it just didn't. He didn't want to marry me. He wanted to marry someone else."

As soon as I started asking my dad questions, our phone conversations got shorter. It was as if he were just ticking off the same list of questions each time: How are you? Have you gotten sick? How is school? Then, after just a couple of minutes, he'd say good-bye. The talks were never deep, and I didn't feel like we knew much of anything about each other. There were no "I love yous" that I can remember. He always seemed to think I was calling because I wanted money, even though I told him that's not why I was calling.

Now that I was turning fifteen, it was more important to me than ever to have a male role model in my life, and I hoped very much that he would show up at my quinceañera. Even though I had given up the fantasy about us having a close father-daughter relationship, I still wished that we could at least know each other better.

My mom helped me plan the party, but we didn't have enough money to pay for everything ourselves, so we asked the family for help. It's customary for there to be several "godfathers" of the party—one godfather who pays for the cake, another who pays for the dress, another who pays for flowers, and so on, and that's how it went in my family. We asked for help, and my family did what they could.

I was so excited when Javier agreed to pay for my cake,

because that was one of the most extravagant touches of the day. Instead of one big cake, I wanted to have sixteen cakes: fifteen small cakes with photographs of me from when I was born through age fourteen, and then one bigger cake with a picture of me now, turning fifteen. The photos would be edible toppers.

My father was supposed to pay for my dress, but he didn't come up with the money, so my mom paid. He had also told me he would buy me a car when I turned sixteen, but I had my doubts (which, of course, turned out to be very reasonable doubts).

The birthday girl's father typically has an important role in the party. He may perform the ritual of the shoe, where he changes the girl's shoes from the flats she arrives in to the heels she'll leave in, to symbolize her transition to adulthood. Both parents walk the girl into the church Mass together to show support and guidance, and then she leaves the Mass by herself to show that she's walking into the world alone. At the party, the father usually gets a special dance. But I was afraid to plan anything around my dad, considering his track record. Instead, I figured it was my mother's right to walk me into church alone because she had played the roles of both mother and father in my life. And my godfathers and brothers would dance with me even if my father didn't show up. I explained to each of them how important this dance was to me, and they nodded their agreement.

My oldest brother, Genaro, would be my "anchor." It was now three years since he'd lost his baby girl, and he seemed to be in a much healthier frame of mind now, and no longer angry with God. He's the one I looked up to most as a father figure and role model. Outgoing and full of energy, he worked hard to go after the things he wanted and had done so many interesting things with his life already. He had joined Job Corps as a teenager to learn how to be a firefighter, and he had traveled to New York and other states to put out fires. I had sure never been to New York or done anything so heroic.

You couldn't keep Genaro indoors; he was the type who needed to be outside and moving. He'd go camping whenever he could. He loved animals and had a soft spot for whatever pets he picked up along the way. I adored him.

I told him that I was worried my father wouldn't show up, and I asked him if he would be the last one to dance with me that night. He said yes.

"This is important to me, Genaro. It's a special honor."

"I know, I know, it's important," he said.

I had only the slightest twinge of worry because of his drinking.

I overestimated him.

On the day of the party, I wore the most beautiful lilac gown. I'm not the kind of girl who dresses up very much, but on this day my sister-in-law did my hair and I wore makeup, leaving my boyfriend awed. Jorge and I had been together for about a year at that point, and he and his brother were also in my court of honor.

We went to our regular church, where the priest said a special blessing for me. I've always had strong faith, which is important to my mother—after all, the name she gave me, Gabriella, means "God is my salvation"—so the priest's words were meaningful. I felt like God was looking down on me and giving his approval as I took my first steps toward womanhood.

After the Mass, my court of honor and I went with the photographer to take pictures. Everyone looked beautiful and I thought things were going really well. When we got to the party, though, I saw that Genaro was already drunk. He's an outgoing guy, but not *that* outgoing. He was being too loud and laughing at nothing, making people feel uncomfortable.

As we sat and ate, Genaro began popping balloons across the room. He thought this was hilarious. We'd blown up lots of balloons to decorate the hall, and there was my adult brother, acting like a rambunctious seven-year-old. Then, randomly, he'd scream out my name or yell something inappropriate. I wanted to hide. It seems there's someone like that in every family, but *why did it have to be him?* Why did it have to be the man I looked up to most?

I had never been embarrassed by my family. My mom's

story doesn't make me look down on her; it mostly inspires me that she's risen above so many obstacles in her life. And I just never thought to feel "less than" because my family didn't always have great judgment when it came to relationships and pregnancy. They were still my family and I loved them. I never felt like their mistakes should be a reflection on me and my character. But this was the first time I felt truly ashamed that my friends were seeing my brother act this way.

When I tried to get Genaro to come out into the hall to practice the dance, he said, "I'm not going to be in the dance. I have to take care of my daughter."

His daughter was sleeping, and one of my sisters was watching her. There was no reason in the world why he couldn't take part in the dance, except that he was drunk and didn't feel like it.

I walked away in tears. The photographer followed me, snapping pictures right in my face as I cried.

"Please go away," I said. "Don't take pictures of me like this!"

"You need to remember every moment of your day," he said.

I was positive that I would remember this, even though I didn't want to.

By the time the dance rolled around, Genaro had disappeared. One of my uncles took his place, wearing a white shirt instead of the lilac one I had picked out for the men in my dance. Seeing the shirt just made it more visual for me that something was *wrong*. On the plus side, my father did show up for the party, so he ended up being the one I danced with last. He didn't make it to the church or the reception, but I was glad he was there at least for a little while.

But it didn't make up for my brother. When he reappeared that night, I avoided him. It was too hard to look at him and feel anything other than anger. All I wanted to do was enjoy the rest of this special day, but now a cloud hung over the room for me. He never apologized—not that day, and not ever after. It was a sad turning point in my life.

I have no male role models left, I thought. He had been the one I thought of like a dad, and this just killed it for me—I hadn't mattered enough for him to quit drinking for even one night. Didn't he see the way I looked up to him? How could he have been so careless about this occasion when he knew how special it was to me? It broke my heart.

"You don't have to live down to the stereotypes people have about you," I had said to him earlier. I knew how he rationalized his drinking: His father was an alcoholic, and people had been telling him his whole life that he was going to be one, too.

"I can't help it. It's in my genes," he'd say.

"You can help it. You don't have to drink."

"It's because he used to drink in front of us all the time. You learn what you see."

"Yeah, but you can choose a different path. Just because people expect something of you doesn't mean you have to give them what they expect. It's your life to live."

My words never sank in. From time to time, both before and after that, he would come to our house and complain to my mother and me about his drinking problem . . . well, when he acknowledged it was a problem. Sometimes he did and sometimes he didn't. There were times when we'd mention it and he'd say, "There's nothing wrong with me! I'm just having fun."

I have to believe that he knows it's a problem now, especially because one of his two daughters is aware enough to say, "Daddy, please don't drink."

For all his talk about how he was a victim because his father drank in front of him, couldn't he see he was playing that same role in his children's lives? Why would he let the cycle continue, when he was so hurt by it himself?

My mother never acted like a victim. It seemed like no matter what life threw at her, she was determined to get back on her feet and live right. I wanted to see that in my brother, but what I see so far is that he's using genetics as an excuse to screw up his life.

Sure, genetics do play a role in alcoholism. You're more likely to be an alcoholic if one or both of your parents are also alcoholics. But that's just one part of the equation; the other part is your behavior. You can't become an alcoholic if you never take a drink. So if you know you're predisposed to addiction because of your family history, then just don't get started, and you'll never find yourself on that path.

Same with any other type of "family curse." If your parents smoke, don't pick up a cigarette. If your parents are obese, work hard to exercise and eat right so you don't follow in their footsteps. But some people find it easier to play the victim. They do whatever bad behaviors or bad habits they want to because they think they have a built-in defense—"I grew up this way."

I have to hope that Genaro will get his act together and become the right role model for his kids. I still believe in him, love him, and want him to get better. But for me, the last dream I had of having a father figure to admire was shattered into fragments on that day.

"You can't stay mad at him," my mother said, weeks later.

"Yes, I can!"

"He made a mistake."

"It wasn't a mistake. He knew how important this was to me, and he decided to get drunk anyway, before we even started the party. How am I supposed to forgive him if he hasn't at least apologized?"

Over time, and partly for my mother's sake, I let some of the anger go, but it still changed me inside. It crystallized a thought I'd been working through for some time: Why do people give in to the stereotypes others have about them?

Why would you ever let someone else's negative thoughts dictate how you're going to live your life?

Already, I'd been fighting the stereotypes myself. Because of my family's history, as soon as I started dating, people would say, "You're going to get pregnant in high school just like Jessica." Jessica was closest to me in age, so that's why they often compared us. Jessica herself liked to taunt me with that—"You're not perfect. You're going to make the same mistakes I did."

"I may not be perfect, but I am nothing like you," I would retort. I expected more from myself, so I worked to achieve it. People told me I had potential, so I believed them. I had never really considered whether Jessica, or any of my other siblings, ever had someone who believed in their potential.

Jessica would tell me I was spoiled, that my mother would buy me anything I wanted, and that I had such an easy life. Had she seen my life? It was strange to imagine that anyone would think of it as a privileged existence. My shoes were three years old. But I guess people see what they see; maybe the real reason she was lashing out at me was that she was angry our mother had never left me.

When we went to church the week after my quinceañera, the priest welcomed us with a big smile and told me how good it was to see me.

"A lot of girls come to church just for their quinceañera,

and then we never see them again. I'm glad you're here."

I didn't have the nerve to tell him that we'd been here all along and he'd just never noticed us before. It was the same church my mom and I had gone to for years, but maybe we blended in to the background. Now he recognized me because he'd done my special ceremony, where I was sitting front and center. Either way, I was glad to have his approval. I remained very involved with the church, participating in different groups and fundraising events, like the annual festival. I was even a candidate for the festival's queen one year.

After church, I'd check to see if my mom needed help watching my nieces and nephews or my grandmother. If not, I'd go out with my friends, maybe to the park, to the mall, out to eat lunch, or to see a movie.

Fifteen didn't feel very different from fourteen. I was still a kid. My friends were still kids. We couldn't drive or vote or go to dance clubs. Even though I was now a woman according to my culture, my heart knew that I still had plenty of growing up to do, and I was in no rush. Being a teenager was something I'd get to do only once, and I wanted to enjoy it.

This is it. This is how it feels to be fifteen.

I was exactly the same age my mother was when she had her first baby.

CHAPTER 5

JORGE

As a teenager, I got more frustrated by the way my siblings would talk to my mom. They treated her with such disrespect and even contempt at times, throwing in her face that she had abandoned them. Nothing she did since then would ever be enough.

Many would take advantage of her. Genaro would "borrow" money frequently, telling her he had no money to pay this bill or that. Except it was borrowing only in the loosest definition of the word—he wouldn't actually pay her back.

"Why do you think she has money? We have bills to pay, too," I'd say. But my mom would hand over another twenty, always with him assuring her that he'd get it back to her. And then, miraculously, his fridge would be stocked with beer.

"Come on, Mom, he's just using you so he can buy alcohol," I'd say.

I was beginning to grow more of a backbone with my siblings. As I became stronger, I wanted to pull my mother up with me. It seemed that she was resigned to always bear the brunt of other people's problems. Even though we were hardly the best equipped to handle it, somehow we were the ones taking care of my grandmother. My mother had seven other siblings, but they each had a reason for not getting involved. Some lived too far away, one was too depressed, another too impatient.

Essentially, my mom was taking care of four generations of people. I wanted my siblings to notice that and appreciate it, and do things for her in return. But I felt like they did the bare minimum more often than not.

Topping it off were their lectures to me. Javier, in particular, was good at criticizing me and telling me what I should be doing.

"You don't know anything," he'd say. "You haven't even lived yet."

I felt like I had something to prove. Just because I was young didn't mean I was stupid. I was tired of always trying to justify myself, and defend myself and my mother to them. That's what was on my mind when I met Jorge.

Jorge was three years older than I was, a senior when I met him at homecoming. A mutual friend introduced us, and at first, although I thought he was very handsome, I was not that impressed. I had seen Jorge around the halls with lots of different girls. He seemed like a ladies' man. But I had a nice conversation with him and we became friends.

Right away, I found that I could talk to him about anything. We went to the park together and talked about our families—I told him about my brothers and sisters, and he told me about his parents. He had wanted to play sports in high school, but he wasn't allowed. His father pulled him off the soccer team after just one week.

"Your responsibility is here with the animals," he said. Jorge's family owned a ranch with chickens and dogs and other animals, and Jorge was expected to take care of them.

"I didn't tell him to buy the animals. They aren't mine, they're his," he said. But he did what his father told him. His family was very traditional Mexican, where the men were expected to take care of the animals and the cars, and the women were expected to cook and clean and take care of the kids.

It surprised me to find more to Jorge than I had first seen. There were so many sides to him, and I always felt good after we spent time together. He made me laugh, and I encouraged him to take school more seriously. He had been considering dropping out because it didn't look like he was going to graduate—his grades were too low, which was his own fault for skipping class so much and not studying.

We sat together in the cafeteria, where he fit in well with my group of friends. Jorge is very laid back but full of energy and a little crazy . . . so it's easy to be around him. He makes people feel good.

After several months, he asked me out and I said yes; he was my first serious boyfriend. I was a bit wary of relationships because I'd seen that most of the ones in my family didn't work out. But I tried to judge Jorge for Jorge, and not for what other men had done or what people had told me about him. He'd dated one other girl for about a year prior to me, but aside from that, his relationships were short-lived. I knew his history, but I also knew that things would be different for us. We were great friends and we respected each other.

Our budding relationship didn't sit well with some of the people around me, like my favorite teacher, Mr. Myers.

"Are you sure about this guy?" Mr. Myers asked me. "He's a lot older than you, Gaby. That's usually trouble."

I liked that Mr. Myers looked out for me. I knew that his concern was genuine because he wanted me to reach my full potential, and it was exciting that he saw such potential in me. I wasn't much of a science student until I took his course in the ninth grade, but he thought enough of me to recommend me for a special University of Washington program taught over spring break . . . and it was one of the best experiences of my life. It gave me a taste of what college would be like, and that got me even more fired up about going to college. I would be the first in my family to go, and I was absolutely determined to make it.

Jorge, on the other hand, found out his fears were right: He wouldn't graduate on time. He hadn't taken his studies seriously, and now he'd have to stay in school for another year if he wanted his diploma. With some encouragement, he decided to do it. I had mixed feelings. Of course I was disappointed that he wouldn't graduate with his class, but on the plus side, at least I'd get to see him around school for another year.

We spent our weekends at the movies, sometimes seeing one after another. We would watch anything, from thrillers to dramas to chick flicks. I know there are lots of guys who wouldn't be caught dead in a Julia Roberts movie, but Jorge is a really good sport. We have fun wherever we are and whatever we're doing.

It took my family some time to come around to Jorge. My siblings didn't bother trying to get to know him in the beginning. They didn't like the idea that I had a boyfriend, period, much less that he was older and repeating his senior year of high school.

"Just stay away from him," Javier said. "You shouldn't be thinking about anything but your studies right now."

"I'm doing really well in school. You don't need to worry about me."

"Gaby, you don't know. Your own future is what you need to think about. You don't need to get it mixed up with this."

All of them except Jessica seemed to consider me the family's "last hope." Javier had been the only other one who did well in school, but becoming a teen dad had limited his options a great deal. They knew I was on the right track, and if Jorge and I were sexually active, that could derail me.

Sonya gave me a hard time about the many quinceañeras we went to every weekend—she thought that meant we were out partying and getting into trouble, but we weren't. It was just something fun to do with friends. She didn't see my day-to-day life, where I had already drifted apart from my main group of girlfriends because they were getting into drinking. It wasn't the path I wanted to be on.

Even when it was insulting at times, I told myself that they were just being protective of me. I felt bad for Jorge, though, because it was disrespectful to him. They didn't take the time to get to know him or us as a couple, to find out that we had a very healthy relationship, to see the good effect we had on each other . . . and to know that we both were responsible for our bodies and our behaviors. Being with Jorge hadn't affected my studies or my interests; I was still working just as hard and staying involved in my church, volunteer activities, and home responsibilities.

After a while, I just wanted them to butt out. Javier's lectures grated on me because they felt so hypocritical. He'd tell me that I didn't know anything about relationships and how to make it work with another person, and yet his own relationship was on the rocks. He made these grand proclamations about what marriage was about, and how "what's his is yours and what's yours is his"—and yet he and his wife kept their finances separate.

To be fair, Jorge's family didn't take to me quickly, either. His mom was worried that I was taking away her son, and his dad was worried about our age gap. He told Jorge, "If you break up with her, she could have you arrested!"

So we didn't start our relationship with much support. Even my mom was worried for the first few months. She thought I would fall head over heels and then this guy would break my heart, so she discouraged me from dating. But as she got to know him, she came around. He's a very handy person who knows a lot about cars, carpentry, electric work, and just about every other useful hands-on pursuit. And he's generous with his skills, which meant that he was the first person to offer to help my mom whenever something went wrong with the house or car.

It didn't take long for her to catch on. "He does more for me than my own kids," she said.

Their relationship grew strong. It's a good thing, too, because she hangs out with us more like a teenage friend than as a mom, and I can't imagine being with a guy who wouldn't embrace that. He goes to church with us and helps with their events, which is nice because he hadn't been to church since a neighbor used to take him when he was little. My mom loves to watch animated movies, so we go to the movies as a threesome. Since her own childhood was cut short, it seems like she's experiencing her teen years for the first time now. I'm glad she feels free to explore her silly side with us.

Once, after it had snowed, we went sledding at a park. My mom climbed up a really big hill and dared Jorge to sled down it. Jorge said no . . . and then my mom hurled herself down the hill, laughing all the way.

"I can't let your mom school me like that," Jorge said, following her.

And that's how it is with them—spurring each other on. Neither of them needs much encouragement. When I met Jorge, he was very into street racing—not among his brightest hobbies. It was hard getting Jorge out of that scene because it was something he enjoyed doing with his friends; it represented a feeling of freedom to him. He didn't like to think about the downsides of it, which were the danger and the expense of speeding tickets.

"That money could be going toward so many other things," I said.

But it wasn't until his friends got into a bad crash that Jorge quit racing. Their car flipped, and it was a miracle they all walked away unharmed. It brought Jorge a dose of reality, which was a relief. I knew better things were in his future. Jorge did graduate from Toppenish High School one year late, and I'll never forget how excited he looked as he received his diploma. My mom and I were so proud of him for sticking to it and achieving his goal.

My own graduation was still two years away. I was just about to start my junior year, where things were heating up in anticipation of college. But I didn't want to wait until then to do something important with my life. I wanted my life to matter now. Somehow, I knew I was going to make a difference.

The only question was how.

PART 2
PREG-NOT

CHAPTER 6

SENIOR PROJECT

A few months earlier, I had been sitting in my biology class—
I was the only sophomore to ever take Advanced Placement
Biology at Toppenish High School—starting lessons about
anatomy and the reproductive system. I had become accus-
tomed to the many seniors who'd come into our classes to
practice their Senior Boards presentations in front of us.
Each senior had a faculty adviser, so they'd come into a class
taught by their adviser to try out their presentation. My biology teacher, Mr. Myers, must have advised a lot of students
because I saw a lot of these presentations in his class.

I'd known about Senior Boards since I was a freshman.
Each senior had to complete a series of tasks as part of their
English requirements. They were each given a thirty-page
packet of information about it when they started the school

year. Among the items in the packet were instructions, suggestions for projects, a letter to our parents in English and Spanish telling them about the assignment, and a schedule of deadlines.

"What do you have to show for yourself after spending the last twelve years in school? A diploma? A career? The Toppenish High School Senior Boards will lead students through one last adventure at THS! It is up to each individual to make it something that will represent their talents and efforts to the community," the cover letter started.

Jorge was working on his senior project that year, so I got to read the instructions and see all the steps he needed to take to pass. My mind wandered to what I might do when my time came.

The requirements stated that we had to pick a topic we had "great interest" in, get it approved by the committee during the early part of our senior year, research the topic to write a six- to eight-page paper, then work with a mentor in school or in the community on a project related to that topic. The mentor could not be a family member. At the end, we had to put together a portfolio of our work, including a multimedia presentation, and give a speech to a panel of community members who would help determine our grade. Practically speaking, it was a chance for students to work on a skill that would be valuable in their careers, to help them prepare for life after graduation.

During the seniors' practice presentations in our classes, they'd talk for ten or fifteen minutes, then we'd ask questions and tell them what we thought they did well and what needed work. For the most part, people researched hobbies that interested them—like massage therapy or dog training or baking. As I mulled over what I might do for my senior project, those kinds of things didn't seem like enough to me. I wanted to do something bigger, something that would have a real impact on the kids in my school. Maybe even on the community.

Baking scones wasn't going to have that impact.

The list of suggestions provided in the information packet included many craft-based skills, like learning how to quilt or decorate a cake; volunteer work that would benefit the community, like starting a children's choir or helping with the Special Olympics or Habitat for Humanity; and practical skills, like carpentry or website design. Some ideas were more general topics that you could think about and figure out how to approach, like teenage depression. Nothing on the list resonated with me.

At the bottom of the suggestion list was a quotation from Canadian graphic designer Bruce Mau's *Incomplete Manifesto for Growth*: "You have to be willing to grow. Growth is different from something that happens to you. You produce it. You live it. The prerequisites for growth: the openness to experience events and the willingness to be changed by them."

That's what I wanted: to find an opportunity for growth, both for me and for the people around me. The statistics told me that my classmates' families were a lot like mine—full of broken homes, teen pregnancy, poverty, and a lack of education. There had to be a project I could do that would reflect our community and make a dent in our problems. But what?

Because of the impact A Child Called "It" and its sequels had on me, I thought I might do something related to foster care. Visit foster kids? Volunteer at an agency? I obviously couldn't take in a foster child, nor could I become one myself, so that topic fell short of what I was looking for. I wanted something I could really immerse myself in, something that would have a long-lasting impact.

It was only fitting that I thought about this in Mr. Myers's class. He was the kind of teacher who really did make a long-lasting impact on his students' lives. He had a personal interest in our success; he would take the time to talk to us before or after class just to ask how we were doing. In class, he encouraged students to ask questions and go on tangents, so our lessons didn't always follow the syllabus. We might start by talking about photosynthesis and wind up discussing the mating habits of spiders. Then he would realize we had just a few minutes left in class and say, "What were we talking about? Oh yes, photosynthesis."

On this day, the topic was human reproduction, so we were learning about how DNA works. One of the students asked whether or not homosexuality was determined by genes, and off we were on a long discussion that covered things only mildly related to our original lesson. It set my mind spinning about all sorts of things, like gay marriage, abortion, nature versus nurture. . . . We even talked about the ethics of modern obstetrics, where couples can now find out in advance if their baby will have a genetic disorder, and often abort the baby if they find out it's so.

That's when the idea came to me . . .

I would fake a pregnancy.

That's what I would do for my senior project. It was a crazy idea, and yet, it felt like the perfect idea. There were so many reasons I wanted to do it. First, it would give me better insight into what my mother and sisters had gone through, as well as all the other teen moms around me. I'd get to see what their lives were like and how they were perceived and treated. Maybe it would give me some understanding into why there are so many sad stories resulting from teen pregnancy—why the mothers don't wind up doing much with their lives, why the kids so often have problems with anger, depression, and substance abuse. It felt like a puzzle I needed to solve.

But on a more personal level, I also wanted to open up a discussion about stereotypes and statistics. Being a Hispanic girl from a family full of teen pregnancies meant that my odds of also becoming a teen mom were way higher than average.

Using Genaro's logic, I could go ahead and give in to that statistic and say it's in my genes to be a teen mom, just like he excuses his alcoholism by saying that's in his genes. It's absolutely true that daughters of teen moms are three times as likely to become teen moms themselves, but why? There's no "you have to have unprotected sex at fifteen" gene.

Generation after generation perpetuates the bad things their families have modeled. We're told that abused kids become abusive adults, so it's somehow more excusable when it happens. ("He couldn't help murdering his coworker; he was abused as a child.") Whatever our parents and grandparents and siblings did becomes what people expect of us—and too many people fall prey to those expectations. There's no reason why abused kids need to become abusive adults. And there's no reason why kids of teen moms need to become teen parents themselves.

I'd been told for so long that I was going to end up just like my sister Jessica. If I gave people what they predicted, how would they react?

My main goal was to make my peers take teen pregnancy seriously—if it could happen to me, it could happen to them—and encourage them to make responsible decisions about their bodies and sexuality. If I could get kids thinking and talking about the subject rather than just tuning out lectures in health class or watching crazy teen pregnancy shows on MTV, maybe it would have an impact.

I also hoped to have a broader reach than just the topic at hand. In my family, the stereotype I struggle against is teen pregnancy, but in other families, it might be problems like drugs or gangs or violence. If I could get my message across right, maybe I could get my peers to think about how to rise above whatever stereotypes people have about them, too.

All of these thoughts buzzed in my mind as I went through the rest of my day with a newfound excitement. The first hurdle would be a tough one to clear, though: I had to get the committee to approve my project. I knew what I was proposing was unconventional, to say the least, and nowhere near as easy to rubber-stamp as the cake-decorating projects.

My first step was to share my plan with Jorge and my mom. They both reacted identically:

"You're crazy."

They didn't understand why I'd want to put myself through the torment of feeling like a social outcast, having people judge me for something I didn't even do. My mother, of course, knew firsthand the feeling that I would probably experience. I'd worked hard to earn my reputation as a very good student and someone with strong morals. Would this wreck what I'd built up over the years? Would teachers see me differently, grade me differently? Would my friends whisper behind my back? What role did others' reactions have on the outcome of young motherhood? If people supported you, would it make a difference? I really didn't know what to expect, but I felt ready to take it on.

"This is going to change your life. Are you really going to be able to pull it off?" my mom asked.

"Yes, as long as no one blows it for me. I'm not telling anyone about this, Mom, so you can't, either."

"What do you mean? Not even your sisters and brothers?"

"No, not even them. That's part of the experiment. I need to see how they react to me when they think I'm pregnant. I'm just going to tell one of them because I need someone to find out what the others are saying and report back to me."

"But . . . Gaby, I can't lie to them."

"Yes, you can."

"I'm not a good liar."

"You're going to have to learn, just for a little while."

"How little a while?"

"Six months."

"Six months?!"

"If I get it approved. A senior project is supposed to be something you work on throughout the year. So my idea is that I'll go through this like a real pregnancy, with my belly getting bigger and bigger as the year goes on, until I reveal the truth at my presentation."

"Oh, Gaby, I don't know about this."

"But you'll support me, right?"

"Of course I will. If this is what you want to do, I still think you're crazy, but I'll support you."

I knew I had to keep this idea as close to the vest as possible. If the wrong person heard about it, the project would be ruined—all it would take was one person to spread the rumor that my pregnancy was fake, and I'd have no social experiment left. I'd have to start from scratch with a new project, no matter how much work I might have put in up to that point. So I decided early that I would tell just a very few people I knew I could trust. And the most difficult decision was about Jorge's family: I didn't want to tell them because I wanted to get an honest reaction from them, as well. But I couldn't have done that without Jorge's approval.

"What do you think about not telling your parents about my project?"

"You mean letting them think you're pregnant?"

I nodded.

"I think they would kill me."

"It's important to gather reactions from everyone in a teen's life. I want to get reactions from parents, too."

"No, I don't want to lie to them."

We argued about it for a little while. I didn't want to make things bad for him, but I thought a big part of the experiment was how much parents' attitudes can affect a teen pregnancy.

The other part of it was that Jorge knew his parents couldn't keep a secret. They'd tell his brothers and sisters, who might then spread it around school.

He finally agreed with me, though it was the only part of the project that still made him uncomfortable. He saw one added benefit that I hadn't considered, too: Since my siblings were convinced he only had sex on his mind when he started dating me, he thought this might show them he'd stick around no matter what. Maybe they would like him more if he proved that he was serious about me and our relationship.

The two closest people in my life were on board, but I didn't want to get too ahead of myself by trying to get the project approved in my sophomore year, so I waited out the summer.

In my junior year, I finally made a best friend. I had plenty of close friends, but until then there wasn't just one girl I really shared everything with. The funny thing is that I'd been in classes with Saida since freshman year; we'd even critiqued each other's writing in class. But we sort of ran in different circles, and I hadn't had any deep conversations with her before. Once we started talking, we found out how comfortable we were with each other. She was a serious student like I was, but also a lot of fun to be around. She didn't mind hanging out with Jorge and me together; there was no "third wheel" type of feeling.

And we were good at teaming up on projects. For one

thing, there had been an organization at our school years earlier called M.E.Ch.A: Movimiento Estudiantil Chicano de Aztlán, which means Chicano Student Movement of Aztlán, the homeland of people from Anahuak. It's a national group that was founded to promote higher education and cultural pride and teach students about the history of Chicanos in America. Saida and I brought it back to our school and became vice president and president, respectively.

She and I didn't have everything in common, though. In the cafeteria, she sat at our table of otherwise all boys. They came to me when they wanted to ask personal questions about girls.

"What does it feel like to get your period?" one of them asked.

"Ewww!" Saida said. "Why do you want to know that? Don't ask her that!"

"It's okay. I don't mind," I said.

They'd ask about tampons or bras or other "womanly" topics. To me, these were natural parts of life and nothing to be embarrassed by. My family had always talked openly about these things—maybe even too openly, because I remember many times hearing, "Oh, you'll understand when you're older" when as a kid I overheard some sexual reference that flew over my head.

One day, one of them asked, "How long after sex can a girl find out if she's pregnant?" He was worried.

"About two weeks," I said. I wondered if his girlfriend was about to become the latest statistic in my project. Luckily, she was not.

I told Saida about my pregnancy project. Her enthusiasm made me decide it was time to pitch my idea. The next time I saw the principal in the hallway, I asked if I could talk to him. He said, "I have time right now. Come with me to my office."

So I did. As determined as I was, I was also a bit pessimistic about my odds. Mr. Greene was a young, involved principal who cared a lot about his students, but in a no-nonsense sort of way. He wasn't out to win popularity contests, and sometimes told students, "I don't need fourteen-year-old friends." So I knew I wasn't going to win him over with my fabulous charm.

I sat down and said, "Mr. Greene, I know that senior projects are supposed to be proposed at the beginning of senior year, but I have a project in mind and I want to know if you might approve it during my junior year."

"What is it?"

"I'm thinking about a project that will explore how people are influenced by stereotypes." I took a breath. "And the way I want to do that is by introducing a false pregnancy. Mine. I want to fake a pregnancy."

He tipped his head to the side and tried to keep a poker face. "Ohhkay . . . tell me what you're thinking."

"I want to test how people will react to me. I think it will teach me about how the environment can influence whether teen moms decide to keep their babies, have abortions, or give them up for adoption or foster care. I'll go to Planned Parenthood to find a mentor so I can make it seem realistic. I would work with my doctor to figure out what symptoms to show and what I need to know about pregnancy."

I gave him as much detail as I could about what I envisioned: I would keep a journal about my experiences, enlist my best friend to listen in on the hall chatter about me, write down the comments people said about me on cards to be read at a school assembly at the end of the year, and talk about why it's important not to follow the negative stereotypes other people may have about you.

"Is your mother on board with this?" he asked.

"Yes, completely. She's going to help me make the belly, because she knows how to sew."

He sat back in his chair and smiled. "I think it's quite an idea."

Score!

"But Gaby, I can't give you a final answer."

Oh.

"I definitely need to check with a couple of people about this, because I can see a lot of complications. . . ."

His voice trailed a bit. "I don't know how people will react to this. There are risks involved for you and for other students. You've considered that, right?"

"Yes."

"And Jorge, too?"

You mean, like, has Jorge thought about the fact that my brothers might beat him up? Yes, we've talked about that one.

But I didn't say that. I just said, "Yes."

"Well, aside from the fact that I need to check with the superintendent, I'm not the one who's supposed to approve senior projects. There's a Senior Boards committee that you'll need to go through to get approval."

"But I don't want a lot of people to know about this, even the faculty. My results will be worthless if it gets out that my pregnancy is fake."

Normally a student would have to submit a letter of intent to the committee of several faculty members, which consisted of two English teachers and other teachers who'd been around long enough to really understand what Senior Boards were about. Then the committee would discuss each project and decide whether or not it was worthwhile, appropriate, and achievable. It was the appropriateness that could have stood in my way.

"Well, okay," he said, thinking. "We'll keep it to as few people as possible, but at the very least, that's going to have to include someone on the district level and a faculty member or two. Let me set up a meeting for you with the head of the Senior Boards committee. Meanwhile, you start working on a letter of intent about your project. And get me signed permission from your mom to show that she approves of this."

The meeting went about as well as I'd hoped. I knew that he could have easily just flat-out refused to let me do this, because the subject and method were so controversial. What I didn't know at the time was that he was worried about more than just the students; he knew the PTA parents might flip out over it, and that the community as a whole might come down on him and the rest of the administration if anything bad happened as a result of this experiment. But he's a strong leader; his main concern really was about me.

Mr. Greene soon pulled me back into his office for a meeting with Le Ann Straehle, a history teacher and the head of the Senior Boards committee. She'd taught my current events class, but I didn't know her well.

"Is this really what you want to do, Gaby?" she asked. She seemed incredulous that I'd choose to do such a thing.

"Yes, I've thought a lot about it."

The more we talked about my family and my motivation, the more excited she got about the idea.

"This is what we started the Senior Boards for twelve years ago—to get students to do important projects that matter, that make a difference to them," she said. "As long as someone at home knows, I'm okay with it."

Mr. Greene really wanted the approval of the superintendent also, but decided he was too busy, so the vice-superintendent would suffice. I worried about that because I thought, "What if I get permission from the vice-superintendent and I go ahead with the project, but once the superintendent catches wind of it, he makes me stop?"

That was something out of my control, so instead I worked on the things I could control. Knowing that it would be a tough decision for the vice-superintendent to make, I wanted to have all the blanks filled in before I proposed the project. I wanted to make it hard for him to say no to me. So I headed off to Planned Parenthood in search of a mentor.

Before going there, I really had no idea what Planned Parenthood did. Sitting in the waiting room with several other teens and young adult women was an uncomfortable experience for me. I looked at the posters on the walls and read the literature around the tables and quickly caught on that this was, among other things, a place where girls went when they wanted to get abortions.

The Planned Parenthood literature was designed to make girls feel okay about getting abortions, by saying things like "Abortion is common. One in three women will experience an abortion sometime in her lifetime." (Not that she'll *choose* an abortion, but that she'll *experience* one, as if it's something that passively happens to her.) Statistics like that are always to be viewed dubiously; it includes women who had to have abortions because their lives were in danger or because the baby had already died in the womb. It also includes women who were raped.

In their description of an abortion, Planned Parenthood explains, "Either a hand-held suction device or a suction machine gently empties your uterus." *Gently empties your uterus?* It appeared they were doing everything they could to make the baby seem nonhuman . . . in fact, they didn't seem to acknowledge there was a baby at all, just some random unwanted matter stuck in the uterus that needed to be sucked out.

I immediately felt defensive; I hoped no one in the room thought I was there to get an abortion. I'm very much pro-life. Did it matter what these total strangers thought of me? Of course not, but it gave me my first taste of what my senior year might be like—where I'd intentionally be sending everyone a false signal that would likely make them judge me more harshly. I knew it might be hard to withstand, but I felt I could as long as there was a good point to it at the end.

After a short wait, a man called me into a conference room and asked me what brought me to Planned Parenthood.

"I'm looking for a mentor for a school project," I started, and explained my idea.

"You're a really brave girl to do that," he said. "I wish I could help, but I don't think we're the right place for you. We don't really deal with teen moms. We're more about preventing pregnancy, and helping young women learn about their options and reach a decision about what to do if they do get pregnant. What it sounds like you need is someone who can coach you about what pregnancy is like and what a teen mom goes through, and for that, I suggest you go to Memorial's Education Center downtown."

"Memorial" was shorthand for Yakima Valley Memorial Hospital. They had a special department for classes on health topics—things like quitting smoking and dealing with cancer. They offered classes about pregnancy and childbirth, so after an initial phone call, I visited the department and met with the woman they suggested, Mary McCracken. She was a teacher there and also at a school that provided classes for teen moms.

Mary was a tall, round-faced woman with graying hair and a gentle smile. I told her about my project and all the reasons I wanted to pursue it, and she said, "Wow. I'd be glad to help you with anything you need."

Because she was not at the hospital full-time, she also asked another instructor there to be "on call" for me in case I ever needed someone and she wasn't around. That instructor was Lori Gibbons, who had graduated from Toppenish High School about ten years earlier. She knew some of my teachers and shared Mary's enthusiasm. I knew I was in the right hands with the two of them.

To start, they provided me with lots of brochures and

pamphlets about pregnancy and answered my preliminary questions about what sorts of symptoms would appear first—aside from the missed menstrual period, of course. Do all women experience morning sickness? How do they deal with it? What happens to a woman's body during pregnancy? What does a woman look like when she's two months pregnant? Three months? Six months?

Not all of my questions had cut-and-dried answers. For instance, I wanted to know about a woman's emotional state from the beginning to the end of pregnancy.

"Well, I can't give you a week-by-week assessment of how all women feel during pregnancy," Mary said. "It's different for everyone. But I can tell you that being pregnant puts women on a roller coaster of emotions."

Because of the flood of extra hormones, women might become more weepy, or more easily angered, or forgetful and unable to concentrate—a state jokingly nicknamed "pregnancy brain." And that's without the added stresses that come along with being an unwed teen mom who's dealing with school, parents, a boyfriend, lack of money, and whatever other variables are in her life. Those kinds of stressors, in addition to the already crazy hormones, could easily lead to depression, anxiety, and rage, which make it harder for her to make rational decisions.

"Thank you so much for your support and enthusiasm about my project," I said to Mary and Lori. "I just want you to know, though, that I don't have it approved yet, so this is still just the planning stage. I'll stay in touch with you and let you know what happens."

They wished me luck and said they hoped to see me soon.

I went home and did my reading, then I visited my doctor, making an appointment with the pretense that I wanted a regular checkup. When the doctor walked in, she said, "You were here not long ago for a checkup. Is everything okay?"

"I'm sorry," I said. "I don't really need a checkup. There's something else I wanted to ask you about today for a school project."

"Okay, shoot," she said.

I told her what I was up to and asked her more questions. I wanted to know how most women find out they're pregnant, and how to plot out my symptoms and my belly growth. We decided that the best way to do it was to figure out when I wanted to reveal my results, and work backward from there. Finally, I felt ready to write my letter of intent.

In it, I explained the steps I had already taken and that I wanted their approval of both my project and my mentor. Then I did something I thought was pretty clever: I inserted a line at the end stating that if they approved my project, they couldn't take back that approval at any time before, during, or after the project.

I wanted that insurance policy. Just as I was signing a contract stating what I would do, and my mother was signing her permission, I wanted them to sign this letter committing to my project, too. It was risky to turn the tables on them, I knew, but I thought it was important. I was afraid that someone might complain, or something might come up in the middle of the project that would make them get nervous and stop me, and then my work would be for nothing.

Off my letter went to Mr. Greene, and then I waited. John Cerna was the vice-superintendent, and he had previously taught some of my siblings. From the impression Mr. Greene gave me, this really could have gone either way. I knew my principal was pulling for me, but he was unsure of the district officials' willingness to open themselves up to scrutiny.

After a few days, Mr. Greene called me into his office. He and Mr. Cerna sat across from me, and they grilled me about my idea and my intentions. I tried to be prepared for anything they threw my way.

"You realize that people may be very critical of you—right, Gaby?" Mr. Cerna asked.

"Yes, I know."

"And how are you going to handle that?"

"Well, I'll know that it's not true, that I'm not really pregnant, so that will protect me. Whatever they say, I'll be able to let it roll off me because there's nothing to take personally."

"Even if it's your friends? What if your friends say really nasty things?"

"I'll be okay. People are always going to talk. . . . You can't live your life afraid of gossip. I have the confidence to know that I can push through anything."

"There's no ulterior motive for this project, right? No one you might be trying to get back at or something?"

"No."

"And when you read the comments that people have said about you at the assembly, I want to make sure you're not going to name names. There shouldn't be any finger-pointing or embarrassing anyone for things that they might have said."

"Definitely not," I agreed. "I plan to have a few people help me read the comments and keep them anonymous. I would just say that these are some of the things people said about me."

"And you understand that people might get mad at you when you tell them the truth?"

"Yes."

As our discussion went on, I thought I could see where it was going, but I wasn't sure until I heard Mr. Cerna say the words: "Gaby, we're going to sign this and approve your project."

Right now?

My heart raced as I watched the men each sign my letter

of intent, as significant to me as watching the president sign an important new bill into law.

This is it, I thought. *It's in pen. They can't erase it. They'd have to use Wite-Out. They wouldn't use Wite-Out, would they?*

A million similarly stupid thoughts went through my mind as they handed me that paper. I thanked them over and over and headed off to class with my mind bursting with electricity and my body unable to contain my enthusiasm. I practically bounced down the hallway, and when I got to class, I couldn't stop dancing in my seat.

Saida was behind me.

"What?" she whispered. "You got it approved, didn't you?"

I smiled and nodded. Then Saida was dancing in her seat, too. The two of us grinned and giggled until the students around us gave us funny looks.

It was really happening now.

CHAPTER 7

THE BIG ANNOUNCEMENT

Jorge drove me home from school that day. I almost burst in two during the car ride, but I waited until he and my mom were together before I told them the news.

"Guess what?" I asked.

"What?"

"I got it approved!"

They were so happy for me. Nervous, but very happy. They knew how much it meant to me.

"This is going to be very big," my mom said. Looking back, that was an understatement.

There were a few reasons I decided that I wanted my "big reveal" to happen at the six-month mark. First, I wanted to get far enough along that I was really "showing" by the end. But I also wanted to end it before the point where most people find out if they're having a boy or girl and people start planning baby showers. And also? I admit it: I didn't really want to look pregnant at my senior prom.

So we decided that I'd come clean in April. The timing of the presentation would mean that I'd have to "get pregnant" in October. Jorge and I looked at the calendar and realized that homecoming was in October—a perfect event to tie in. So that would be the big night. I'd tell everyone I got pregnant the night of the homecoming dance.

Aside from my mother, the only other person in the family I told about the project was my sister Sonya. My family had nicknamed her "The Information Superhighway" because she's the one who talks most to everyone else in the family, so I figured she'd be a good person to spread the news and gather their reactions for me. When I told her, she burst out laughing.

"Oh, that's a good one!" she said. "They're going to freak out. I can't wait to see their faces when I tell them!"

She's the first person who actually saw humor in the situation, but that's Sonya. She laughs at everything.

Back at school that September, there was a great surprise waiting for me: Mr. Cerna had been promoted. He was now the superintendent. My last obstacle, gone! I no longer had to worry that someone higher up in the district was going to come along and squash my project. I felt like a pilot on a runway being told, "You are cleared for takeoff."

I read all the booklets my doctor gave me and consulted pregnancy websites like BabyCenter.com, where you could follow your baby's development from week to week to find out what was happening, from conception to birth and beyond.

When October came around, Mr. Greene started joking with us in the hallways. "Two weeks till the big day!" he said. Jorge and I went to the homecoming dance knowing that this was my last night as a normal, "unpregnant" teen. The next day, my method acting began.

Of course, after all that planning, there wasn't actually much to do for the next month or so. It was a little anticlimactic to be carrying around this secret of what was to come but not be able to actually drop any hints yet. It was too early for me to show symptoms, and I certainly wouldn't know I was pregnant yet. Instead, I spent my time reading and studying so I'd know exactly what was supposed to be happening to my growing fetus.

It wasn't until late November that I was able to plant the first seeds. A friend of mine asked me if I had a tampon, and I said no. "You know, it's funny," I said. "Now that you mention it, my period is late."

"Oh, it's probably nothing to worry about," she said. "Your period might just be switching its time of the month. That happened to me. It used to come at the beginning of the month, and now it comes at the end."

"Yeah, you're probably right," I said.

My mentor, Mary, let me take classes at the education center for free. There were usually seven to ten pregnant girls in each class. Most were teens, some in their twenties. Jorge came with me to the classes, and looking around the room, that made me feel really sad for some of the girls. Some were there with their moms or another family member, but no guy in sight. Here I was, just faking a pregnancy, and my boyfriend was still willing to sit through hours of these classes with me to be supportive.

I was already better off than most pregnant teens. Eighty percent of teen dads don't marry their baby's mom, and they pay on average less than eight hundred dollars a year in child support, according to the book *Kids Having Kids*, edited by Saul D. Hoffman and Rebecca A. Maynard.

Why do so many guys bail? And why does society let them?

We sat at large tables and listened as the instructor taught us about how to have a healthy pregnancy. We would watch videos that showed a baby's development through each month. I learned what to eat and what not to eat, and when the baby's hearing and lungs would develop, and what kinds of chemicals to avoid—like paint fumes and harsh cleaners.

For the most part, all the girls kept to themselves and whomever they were with. There weren't a lot of side conversations or bonding between us, so I was left to wonder what their stories were and how scared they might be of what was to come.

In one class, the instructor had the men try on a fake pregnancy suit: a full-body prosthetic that included an accurately weighted belly and fake pregnancy boobs. The idea was for the men to find out what their girlfriends or wives felt like all day, carrying around this extra weight and being wobbly and off-balance because of the uneven distribution of that weight.

"Man, this is too heavy!" Jorge said. "This would really stink. I don't know how any woman does this."

Mary offered to let me borrow one of the suits for my project, but I declined her offer. Because it was made for men to try on, it was too large for me, and I didn't want to deal with the padded fake breasts, which would limit what I could wear and probably look too obvious.

In the beginning, I didn't need any sort of fake belly. It takes a while for women to show, and when they do at first, it's small enough that I could just wear extra layers of clothing and stick out my belly. That's what I did starting in December. I'd wear sweatpants and oversized shirts with extra T-shirts underneath, bunching them up around my middle. And I started complaining of nausea. My first symptom!

Normally I ate breakfast at school with a table of my friends, but starting in December, I ate my breakfast at home and then sat at the cafeteria table and tried to look queasy.

"Ugh, I can't even look at food. I feel so nauseous," I'd say.

Saida would make comments to make sure people heard what I was saying. "You're nauseous again? What's wrong with you?"

"It's probably just something you ate yesterday that didn't agree with you," a friend said.

"Yeah, maybe," I said.

I had the dates plotted out on my calendar at home, and December 6 was the day I had decided I was going to find out I was pregnant. After that date, Saida changed her comments to drop hints that she knew.

Now when I came in and said I felt ill, she'd say, "Gaby, you have to eat something! It's important."

"I know, I know," I'd say.

"Especially *now*," she'd say with added meaning, and shoot me a look. I'd glance back at her seriously, a silent bit of acting to show we had a secret.

And when we were moving around boxes to prepare for a student assembly, she'd say, "You shouldn't lift that. Give that to someone else, or I'll take it for you."

Jorge noticed that the women in the pregnancy classes kept leaving the room to go to the bathroom, so he suggested that to me—"You need to go to the bathroom a lot more often." I wasn't sure how early to start that, but it turns out pregnant women have an increased need to pee almost immediately after conception, because of the increase in hormones and the fact that the uterus is expanding. So I plotted out my pee schedule, too—I tried to leave each class two or three times per week to go to the bathroom.

I thought it would look silly if I left each class every single period, so I staggered it so that if I went to the bathroom during one class, I didn't also excuse myself in the next. I thought that would be too over-the-top for the students who were with me in consecutive classes.

I'd just raise my hand and ask to be excused.

"*Again?*" one of my teachers asked in exasperation.

"Sorry, I just really need to go."

After a week of these funny behaviors, some of my friends did at least say, "What's wrong with you?" and suggest that I see a doctor about all my stomach problems. No one even hinted at taking a pregnancy test, though. I got a little frustrated that they didn't seem to recognize my symptoms or Saida's overprotective comments, but maybe I wouldn't have, either. Or maybe they were just too afraid or polite to voice the obvious possibility. After all, I had lectured some of them about safe sex and abstinence; maybe they were hesitant to confront me about my own behaviors.

My act for about the first ten days was that only Saida and Jorge knew I was pregnant. I made a big point of choosing lots of fruits and vegetables on the lunch line to show people that I was eating healthier now, and Saida and Jorge encouraged that. They would make comments like, "Are you getting enough vegetables?"

Then, in mid-December, it was time to start telling people. I was tremendously nervous about that step. Was I a good enough actress? How would I handle their questions? What if someone asked me something that really stumped me? I had tried to learn everything I could—what I should be feeling at that point, what was going on with the baby, what my first doctor's appointment would have been like—but I still felt like there might have been other things that only a pregnant woman would know.

The first person I told was my fitness teacher, Mr. Piper, because I was taking an intense performance-training course and didn't want him to find out from someone else and then think I was working out too much in class because I wanted to lose the baby. So I just came out with it before class one day: "I need to tell you that I just found out I'm pregnant."

"Okay," he said with a look of concern. "How are you doing?"

I tried to look neutral. "Fine," I said. It was important that I not influence their reactions by looking depressed or nervous or happy or anything in particular. I wanted their honest reactions, unaffected by what they could read on my face.

He asked a few more questions to make sure I was okay

and then said, "Well, we'll just have to modify what you do here. You can stay in the class, but you'll have to take it easier."

"I'll do whatever you tell me."

"Can you talk to your doctor to create an exercise plan? That way I'll know we're not overdoing it."

"I can do that."

That wasn't as hard as I expected, I thought.

But I was extremely nervous about telling the next teacher: my Associated Student Body (ASB) Leadership club adviser. There were rules about being in the leadership club—you had to show the character and characteristics of a good leader. I wasn't sure if being pregnant was going to disqualify me.

Other students who had been in the club warned me that it got very personal. "We talked about everything in there," one of my friends said. But that's just what I needed, a place to feel comfortable talking about my experiences and hearing about what other people were going through, too. You didn't have to be an honors student to join, or even an upperclassman, although upperclassmen did get priority. You just had to sign up for the leadership class, and the teacher would interview the applicants and choose which ones she thought were right for the group. I was proud to be in the class and it was a meaningful experience for me; I didn't want to leave it but I expected I might have to.

On top of that, Mrs. Dorr was someone I really looked up to on a personal level, and I didn't want to disappoint her. When I approached her and told her that I was pregnant, she said, "Well, I don't see why you can't be a leader *and* a mom."

In that one sentence, she gave me such a feeling of empowerment. It was the best reaction I could have hoped for.

But the third person I told—that's where it got tough.

Mr. Myers, my science teacher, was the third person. He'd been my teacher since freshman year, and he really mattered to me. He had given me such encouragement through the years; he made me feel smarter than I thought I was. We'd had many talks where he gave me fatherly advice, and now, standing in front of him after class, about to tell him this huge lie, I felt . . . terrible.

"I'm pregnant," I said, and the tears started overflowing. I cried because of guilt, because I hated lying to him and knowing that he was going to believe me and *care*. The "fun" of the project had just turned a corner into something else. I couldn't control the unexpected tears, which, of course, only added to the effect. He thought I was crying about the pregnancy. And that made me feel even worse.

I could see the disappointment in his eyes. He didn't have to say anything. Every word out of his mouth was caring and supportive, but I knew how upset he was that it was *me* telling him this.

"Oh, Gaby, are you okay?" he asked.

I nodded.

"Have you seen a doctor?"

"Yes. He said I'm six weeks along and everything is fine so far."

"Have you told your mom?"

"Yes."

"And what is she saying about this?"

"She's disappointed, but she supports me."

"Do you have any fears about this?"

"Well, yeah," I said. "I'm worried about the support I'm going to get from my family, besides my mom. The way things are now, I don't know how my brothers and sisters are going to take this. I haven't told most of them yet."

That was the truth. I was thinking of the way I felt when I recently asked them for help. I had been accepted into a University of Washington course that would allow me to get five college credits while still in high school, but it cost three hundred dollars. My mom couldn't pay it, and I asked my brothers for help. They went back and forth with it and finally turned me down, saying, "If you can't afford it, why are you taking that kind of class?"

It hurt. "Why do you push me so hard to succeed, and then when I do something to move forward, you tell me to pull back?"

It was Javier who stepped up to help me in the end. He

had hoped there would be another option, but when there wasn't, he helped me pay for the course. I was disappointed that none of the others were willing to kick in, considering how many times they'd told me, "If you ever need us, we're here for you!" I wondered if it was all just talk.

Mr. Myers knew so much about me already. There were just a few teachers who I'd opened up to about my home life. He was one I could always go to about anything—when I was worried about my grandmother, or upset by something my brothers had done, or just stressed about a test. So I knew he wasn't surprised that I was insecure about my family's support.

"How about Jorge? Is he okay?"

"Yeah, he's okay. We'll get through it."

"It's a stumbling block to be sure, Gaby, but it doesn't have to be the end. You can still follow your dreams and have a good life; this just means you have to work harder."

He was trying so hard to be encouraging, even though I could see him envisioning my potential slipping away. I couldn't wait for this to end. I wanted to say, *Don't be sad! I'm just kidding!* But instead I left after a few minutes, and composed myself before heading to the next class. I hadn't expected it to be that painful. I didn't think it would feel like a betrayal because, after all, I was doing it in the name of science. This was to be an important social experiment, the kind of thing that he would love and support . . . except I wasn't including him on it.

That turned out to be the hardest part, the sense of guilt over excluding people. The guilt over lying to them and knowing that they were going to find out there were a few people "in on it" all along . . . just not them.

A couple of people made it easier on me, though, like my friend Nestor. He's an upbeat guy with such a light-hearted spirit, and it was no different in this case. When I told him my news, he giggled a bit and said, "Are you serious?" When I said yes, he actually got excited and told me I'd be a great mom. He asked when I was due (July 27), and if I'd name the baby after him (no). No tears were exchanged this time.

Another friend, who's sort of the polar opposite of Nestor, said, "You're dumb. That was a really big mistake."

Once I told them, some of my friends acknowledged that they were suspicious because of my morning nausea and Saida's comments. Some said they were totally oblivious to that and didn't see this coming. I was glad, at least, that some of my close friends were very surprised to hear I'd gotten pregnant. It meant that not everyone expected me to follow in my family's footsteps.

"You? No way. You're the last person who would get pregnant in high school," my friend Blanca said. "You're the one who's always telling us to be careful and not to mess up our future."

"Well, it happened," I said. It's true—I was always lecturing friends about staying safe, so I wondered if anyone would think I was a hypocrite or if they'd assume my birth control failed.

"What are you going to do?"

"I don't know. What do you think I should do?"

"Whatever you think is right."

No one ever said the word "abortion" out loud, or even "adoption." No one wanted to be the one to make such a suggestion, or to take any sort of stand about what I should do. Over and over I heard the question "What are you going to do?"—but no follow-through advice.

Some people were more willing to ask my best friend the blunt questions, like "Is she going to keep it?" "Of course she is," Saida would say.

For the most part, the teachers asked if I'd seen a doctor and if I was healthy and taking care of myself and eating right. Several asked if I needed anything or if I wanted to talk. One just gasped and didn't say anything else. Most didn't know what to say after those first couple of "checking in" questions.

After class, Saida heard one of the teachers say to a student, "Doesn't she know she just ruined her life?"

It hurt—and I didn't even know why. I *hadn't* ruined my life, but it still didn't feel nice to hear that someone thought I had. Teen pregnancy is not an easy road to go down, and I think it's extremely important to discourage it, but I also don't think anyone has to think of his or her life as *ruined* at sixteen. Harder, absolutely, but "ruined" makes it sound like there's nothing good left in it and no purpose in trying to better yourself. No hope.

But that was the overall sentiment. If I had to pick one reaction that summed up what most people said about me, it's "She ruined everything."

"Now she won't go to college."

"Oh well, it was bound to happen."

"Her life is over."

"I wonder if she'll even graduate."

But I was still me, wasn't I? Pregnant or not, I was still in school and still getting great grades. I was in the top 5 percent of my class, with a 3.8 grade point average. With everything they knew about me, why would they be so quick to write me off as just another statistic?

There were a few people who encouraged me to continue with my studies and told me they knew I could still succeed, but there were far more who said things—mostly behind my back—that were really discouraging.

If I were really pregnant, how would I take these messages?

I thought about my brother Genaro and his slide into alcoholism, telling us that he couldn't help it because it was in his genes. But more than that, it was what people expected of him, and that made it easier for him to give in to it.

I wondered how many of the grim statistics about teen

moms are unavoidable, and how many are the result of the limits other people project on them.

There's a classic example of the four-minute mile: Until 1954, people thought it was impossible to run a mile in under four minutes. No one in recorded history had ever done it, and experts decided the human body just wasn't capable of that kind of speed. Then twenty-five-year-old medical student Roger Bannister did it in 1954.

He later said, "Doctors and scientists said that breaking the four-minute mile was impossible, that one would die in the attempt. Thus, when I got up from the track after collapsing at the finish line, I figured I was dead."

Six weeks after Bannister achieved this historic milestone, so did his rival John Landy. Then another runner, and another, and another. By the end of 1957, sixteen runners had beaten the four-minute mile. It was like Bannister had broken down a wall of impossibility. Suddenly, it was possible. And because the other runners now knew it was possible, they were able to achieve it, too. They no longer had people telling them they couldn't do it.

Why do we insist on putting limitations on what people are capable of doing?

As the days went on before Christmas break, I didn't have to tell many more people my news. As expected, it traveled through the grapevine fast. People would get very quiet when I walked into a room, pretending not to see me. I knew they'd just been talking about me. Sometimes I overheard things; sometimes Saida did.

"I can't believe she was so irresponsible."

"Her boyfriend's going to bail."

I'd been so sure of myself in Mr. Greene's office, telling him and Mr. Cerna that these comments would just roll right off me. But when it actually happened, it was a lot harder to brush off than I thought. I grew defensive. It's a lousy feeling to walk around all day knowing that people are gossiping about you, judging you, predicting that you have no future because you were stupid. I couldn't help but take things personally. These were my friends. Didn't they believe in me enough to know that, even if I were pregnant, I'd still find a way to go to college and achieve my dreams for me *and* my baby?

"Well, at least it won't be a big deal in her family," a friend said to Saida. "They're used to teen moms."

Yeah, right.

CHAPTER 8

UPS AND DOWNS

Let me put it to you this way: Christmas 2010 sucked.

Normally, Christmas is a wonderful holiday in our family. All my brothers and sisters and nieces and nephews are together. When I was a kid, we'd get together at my grandmother's house on Christmas Eve and go to the ten o'clock Mass, and then stay up to open presents at midnight. But as the family grew and grew and each of my siblings wanted to spend Christmas morning with their families, our tradition changed. A few days before, we'd get together at Javier's house, and on Christmas Eve, Sonya would throw a party for anyone who wanted to attend. We may not have a lot of money, but we have each other, and good food, conversation, and laughter. But not that year.

It was just a week or so after my brothers and sisters

found out my news. Of all my siblings, Javier was the one whose reaction I feared most—I knew he was going to be mad—so I chickened out and made Sonya do it. She told him before work one day. He yelled, "What the fuck?" Then he was silent for a long time.

After that, Sonya said, he seemed really sad and defeated. "She had a chance and she just tossed it away. She threw her life in the garbage," he said. "I thought she had learned from our mistakes. She was supposed to be the one who was different and would make our mother proud. She's so stupid."

I learned that, after their talk, Javier moped around feeling guilty that he hadn't done more to stop my relationship with Jorge—not that he hadn't actually tried, of course. He was plenty insulting to both of us, and always full of lectures and unsolicited advice about our relationship. But now he felt like he should have stepped in as an authority figure and basically forbidden me to date, or kept Jorge away from me.

Javier didn't call me. He was waiting for me to call him so he could chew me out, but I didn't give him the opportunity. I ran into Tony at a Walmart, but I didn't feel right announcing my big news—even if it was fake—in the middle of a Walmart checkout line. He later told me that he'd already heard by that point, but similarly didn't want to talk about it there. The news traveled fast until they all knew. And they told my older nieces and nephews, who were not very good at concealing their curiosity. They kept staring at my belly.

My brothers were not kind. They made nasty comments about me to Sonya and to my mom, and one threatened, "If Jorge bails, I'm going to beat his ass."

At our Christmas celebration at Javier's house, there was a completely different mood hanging in the air from usual. It felt like a funeral to me. People were flat-out ignoring Jorge and me—we'd hear them talking and laughing, and then as soon as we came into a room, they'd go silent and sit there with straight faces. My mother walked around wringing her hands, desperate to tell her kids the truth. As much as it would have broken the tension for me, too, I just looked at her seriously and said, "You can't."

My sisters and brothers weren't even making eye contact with us. Jorge was used to it—they'd been ignoring him for years, observing him rather than interacting with him—but it really got to me. The only one who would have anything to do with me was Jessica, which was the biggest shocker of all.

"Just try to enjoy your pregnancy," she said. "Have fun with it."

I waited and waited for an "I told you so." How many times had she said I was going to end up pregnant just like her, and I said, "Never!" Wasn't this her moment of victory, where she got to gloat that she was right and I wasn't morally superior after all?

"I love you, whether you're pregnant or not," she said, and I swallowed hard. I remembered how they had all ignored her when she came back from Mexico. I remembered being the only one still talking to her then, and now here we were, roles reversed so many years later. It seemed like a lifetime in between. I couldn't remember the last time I told my sister I loved her. But I felt like I knew what it was like to be her. Ostracized.

We went through the motions of the holiday without any of the feeling behind it, and then it was over. No one outright yelled at me; they just shot me dirty looks and wouldn't greet me or kiss me good-bye. I was a nonperson.

Jorge wasn't faring any better with his family. In fact, he might have gotten it worse than I did.

He didn't have the nerve to tell his parents, so he just waited for them to find out on their own. Since one of his sisters was in our school, it didn't take long for word to travel to her, and then to his parents. Although Jorge had moved into his own apartment after graduating from high school, he still visited his parents a lot. On one of his visits, they confronted him about it.

"Is Gaby really pregnant?" his dad asked.

He couldn't look at them. He looked away and said, "Yeah."

As soon as he said it, his mother stormed off to the kitchen and wouldn't come out. His father said, "You messed up. Boy, you messed up."

After that, neither of them spoke to him for a week. He was so upset, but he stuck to the story. When they did start speaking to him again, they were not at all accepting of the situation. Jorge heard it from every angle: his parents, his siblings, and especially his friends.

Every time he would see his friends, they'd start in on him all over again.

"Jorge, you really screwed up this time."

"Now you have to stay with her."

"Now you better get a real job."

The next time we visited his parents together, they took us aside. His father said, "Congratulations, and be prepared. . . . You've just made your life way harder. You're trapped now, and you're not going to be able to have fun. Are you still going to college?"

"Yes," I said.

Jorge was working in the Chinese food stand of a local Safeway at the time. After high school, he had wanted to apply for an apprenticeship program to learn how to be an electrician, but there were no openings that year. The following year, he didn't score high enough on the test to get into the program. So he's been studying and biding his time at whatever jobs he can pick up in the meantime, until he's allowed to take the test again next year.

At Safeway, one of his most loyal customers was my principal, Mr. Greene, who loves Chinese food. Whenever Mr.

Greene came in, he'd check on Jorge, and I know his concern was genuine.

"How are you doing with everything?"

"Okay, I guess."

"How are Gaby's brothers taking it?"

"Well, they haven't killed me yet."

I didn't think they would actually do anything to Jorge. They talk big and threaten, but when it came down to it, I didn't think they'd want to harm either one of us. At least, that's what I was counting on.

I couldn't wait to get back to school after Christmas break. School was always the safe place for me—the place where I could just focus on me and not have to worry about the rest of my family.

So I went back to class, ready to focus on my work again . . . but it was not the same sanctuary anymore. I had hoped that once the initial news set in, people would get caught up in the next bit of juicy gossip and not be so concerned with me anymore, but it really just amped up.

"How come you're wearing sweatpants all the time now? Are you getting fat?" someone asked me.

"It's just comfortable."

"It's okay if you're getting fat."

"Yeah . . ."

Had she not heard that I was pregnant? It was so awkward

wondering. Then my own self-consciousness took over and I wondered, "Am I really getting fat?"

A female member of Jorge's family said, "You're getting pregnancy boobs. Your boobs are getting bigger."

"You think?"

I hadn't changed an inch. I was, in fact, more conscious of my weight now. I wanted there to be an obvious difference when I did my big reveal and took off my fake belly in April, so I was making sure to exercise and eat right.

And after a few weeks where I didn't do anything to the number of layers I was wearing, the same female relative said, "You're getting so huge all of a sudden!"

It was hard feeling insecure all the time, realizing that people were scrutinizing everything about me, from my looks to my behaviors. If I was having a bad day, they'd automatically think it was because Jorge dumped me or I was scared about the baby. If I was absent from school, would they think I was dropping out? I felt like people were just watching and waiting for me to fail in some way. If my grades slipped, they could say, "See? I knew she couldn't make it now."

There were, of course, several people who reacted with genuine concern for me, not just the baby. As important as it is to worry about the baby, it's also so important to support the mom—because her emotional state affects the baby. There's some proof that a woman's troubled emotional state can negatively affect the fetus's development in the womb. But on a more concrete level, it definitely affects the baby once he or she is born: If the mom feels depressed and unsupported, how is she going to do a good job of taking care of her baby? Depressed moms don't take care of themselves, let alone their kids. They end up resenting their kids and often not bonding with them, which means the kids don't feel safe and loved.

I wondered how much that had affected my mom and sisters.

One of the teachers who was most supportive of me was my Spanish teacher, Mr. Gonzalez. His wife was pregnant at the time, which just made me nervous. I felt like he was going to see right through me if I didn't know something that she was going through, or if my symptoms didn't match up with hers. After classes, he would always ask me how I was doing, how far along I was, how the doctor's appointments were going. . . . It was hard to look him in the eye, and I usually tried to rush right out of there. I was sure he had X-ray goggles that could see right into my lying little soul.

One day, he offered me some barbecue chips after class.

"Oh no, I can't eat those. I get heartburn," I said.

"Don't worry!" he said. "My wife gets really bad heartburn, too, but these don't bother her."

Hmm. I felt stumped. I had purposely been avoiding spicy foods, as well as fish with high mercury levels, as part of my "what pregnant women shouldn't eat" regimen. But if his pregnant wife ate it, did that mean I was breaking a pregnant woman bonding code if I still refused?

"Uh, no, that's okay," I said. "I'm trying to be really careful."

"So, are you going to find out if it's a boy or girl?"

"No, I want it to be a surprise."

"You're crazy! How are you going to know what to buy, then? How will you know how to decorate the room and what clothes to have ready and all that stuff?"

"I'll just pick neutral things for the beginning. What about you?"

"We're going to find out as soon as we can."

That was one of the main reasons why I didn't want to announce if I was having a boy or girl; I was afraid people might buy little outfits or other presents once they heard.

Of course, Mr. Myers also continued checking on me all the time, reminding me that I wasn't just living for myself anymore and that I had to make sure I was taking care of my health for my baby's sake. He'd ask about my doctor's visits, too, wanting to know how the baby's development was going.

In one of the luckiest turns of events, I was able to add another layer of believability to my project when the head of the Senior Boards committee, Mrs. Straehle, found out she was pregnant. Most ultrasounds are printed with the woman's name and due date and other personal details, but hers weren't. It was perfect: She was really due just before I was pretending to be, which meant that she could pass her ultrasound pictures to me and I could show them around a couple of weeks later, passing them off as my own.

And that's just what I did, showing them to students who were positive they could tell it was a boy or girl. Nestor and Blanca gave the baby ridiculous nicknames that they decided were gender-neutral. Baby Gumbo is the one that stuck.

"If you have Baby Gumbo early, and it's a girl, can I take her to the prom?" Nestor asked.

Barely a fetus and already I had to worry about her dating.

Jorge, too, provided some moments of levity. He and I love to play-fight with each other, but he really made some jaws drop at church one day when we were joking around and he pretended to punch me in the stomach.

"Jorge! You can't do that anymore!" I whispered.

"Oh yeah," he said. "Sorry."

It was like a movie scene where everyone is quiet and every head is turned. He made another gaffe when we were playing ball with a group of people. I missed a ball and he said, "Why didn't you dive for it?"

Duh.

This fake pregnancy thing was taking some getting used to.

By February, I learned in pregnancy class, my imaginary

fetus already had fingerprints and could suck its tiny thumb, even though it was only three inches long—"about the size of a medium shrimp," according to BabyCenter.com. We watched all sorts of videos in class, including one that showed three live births—up close and in living color. It didn't shock me because I had actually seen a real birth: I was there in the hospital when Nievitas was in labor with her youngest daughter. It was a long and very difficult delivery, and the baby ended up weighing ten pounds. That experience alone was enough to make sure I didn't get pregnant for the next ten years. Maybe twenty.

But watching his face during the video, I thought Jorge might pass out.

"Oh, man! That looks so painful!" he said. He turned pale and contorted his face, and I'm pretty sure it meant, "I can't believe I came here with you. I'm scarred for life."

He was waiting for his friends to ease up on him, too, but they didn't. When they weren't taunting him and reminding him of how much he "messed up," they were asking him about how he was going to support us and whether or not I'd applied for WIC (Women, Infants, and Children), a federally funded program that provides a monthly stipend for nutritious food to pregnant women and women with young kids who meet income guidelines.

Even my own brother put me down to him. "You think you want what she's got, but she's gonna feed you to the lions, boy," Javier said. He was speaking about his own experience, of course. He couldn't conceive of the idea that maybe we'd just want to stay together and be happy with each other. Only some of our close friends could. All around us were messages of doom: *You're trapped. You're stuck. You're never going to make it together. You're going to be broke. She's going to suck you dry. This is your ball and chain. You're never going to have any fun again.*

And it suddenly became clearer why so many young men *do* bail.

Jorge couldn't stand it. He wanted everyone to just back off and leave him alone. He didn't want to answer their questions and take all the insults, but it seemed that it was a major topic of conversation every day. People just had to keep reminding him of how terrible his life was going to be from now on. If he had been a real teen dad-to-be, what would those messages have done to him? He wouldn't have had the comfort of knowing it wasn't real and that it would all be over in a few months. Would he begin associating his future baby with a lifetime of unhappiness? If so, it would take an awfully strong man to stick around.

Jorge wasn't in school anymore, so he didn't have teachers to check on him like I did, and none of his friends joked about baby nicknames and taking our baby to the prom. It was just all negativity, all the time.

The thing is, I understand where the negativity comes

from. People say these things because they've seen other young, unmarried parents mess up their lives. It would be unrealistic to expect everyone to say "Congratulations!" and cheer about it—and that would probably be harmful to others, because other teens might see the positive attention and want some of it for themselves . . . leading to more teen pregnancies.

No matter what, I knew that the focus had to stay on avoiding teen pregnancies in the first place. But once the act is done, why throw teen parents under the bus? Whether a committed couple's birth control failed or someone got drunk at a party and had a one-night stand, the result is the same: There's going to be a baby. What good does it do anyone to sit around insulting the parents? What positive result can possibly come of it?

If anything, it becomes a self-fulfilling prophecy. Teen moms don't usually stop at one child. You'd think that they'd have hard lives and never want to get into that predicament again, but it often doesn't happen that way. One in four teen moms gets pregnant again within two years. They wind up having second and third kids without being in solid marriages, but why? Maybe it's because they've been told they're screwups and that their own lives are over now anyway, so they figure this is all they can do in life. Maybe they become more desperate for affection because they've been so ostracized. I can't be sure what goes on in everyone's minds, but I can make guesses based on how I felt during the experiment.

What I felt was that pregnancy was stealing my entire identity. All anyone wanted to talk about was the baby. It was like I was just a human incubator now.

It brought Jorge and me closer because we went through it together, weathering the insults, the gossip and stares, and the disapproval of our families. Lots of times I just wanted to get away with him and be somewhere we wouldn't be judged.

A message board post from a teen mom echoed what I was feeling. "When you get pregnant as a teenager, a lot of people give up on you and treat you like garbage, no matter how smart or nice or hard-working you were before," she wrote. "Nobody wants to 'encourage teen pregnancy,' so they feel it's their duty to make you suffer. It is painful and scarring and it's why a lot of teen moms drop out."

I believe that once the news is announced, the focus needs to be on *what now?* For the benefit of society, it's in everyone's interest to make sure this baby doesn't grow up to become a criminal, or a lifelong welfare recipient. It's entirely possible for the children of teen moms to do great things—you don't need to look any further than President Barack Obama for proof of that. His mom was eighteen when she had him. Or Eric Clapton, Oprah Winfrey, or even Justin Bieber and Selena Gomez—all were reared by teen moms, and no matter what you think of them, they're all hugely successful in their fields.

So why not focus on that? Why not see President Obama's mom as the four-minute mile of teen pregnancy? If she was able to finish her education, attain a successful life, and have one of her children grow up to become president of the United States, then we know it's possible. With enough support and encouragement, maybe the teen dads would stick around, and maybe the teen moms would finish their education, get better jobs, and stop repeating the cycle.

We don't win this battle by finger-pointing and gossiping. We win it by educating, talking, and lifting each other up. We win it by being decent to one another.

CHAPTER 9

THE BUMP

Around February was when my mom made "the bump." We had studied videos, pictures, and real pregnant bellies to figure out just what mine should look like, and we finally settled on half a basketball as a mold. My mom and I went to a craft store to get wire and clay, which she used to build the fake belly around the basketball, then removed the basketball once the clay dried. I fitted it around my abdomen, but the clay was too hard—not like a real pregnant belly would be. Pregnant bellies aren't soft like regular skin, though, so we didn't want to make it out of fabric and stuffing or anything like that. My mom decided to put a thin layer of cotton batting over the clay so it would have a little give in case people touched it, and we stuffed cotton underneath it to make it stick out more.

We had some trouble figuring out how to get me in and

out of this contraption. Should it have a zipper in the back? Snaps? Would people notice that under my clothes? Finally Mrs. Straehle gave me one of her belly bands—a stretchable, supportive fabric that pregnant women sometimes use so they can wear their regular clothes longer and not have to buy maternity clothes right away. They just leave their old pants unbuttoned and unzipped, with the belly band underneath to hide underwear and skin. It also hides the gap if a shirt is too short or hangs out. The belly band turned out to be the perfect way to secure my fake belly. I would just pull the belly up onto my body and then put the band over it to keep it snug.

Luckily, I'm not the kind of person who normally wears very tight or revealing clothing, so I was able to wear the most oversized of my normal wardrobe. I couldn't afford maternity clothes, but I found that a zip-up sweatshirt looked just right over my bump.

Jorge was very picky about making sure it looked exactly right before we debuted my new look. Finally, after all the molding and sculpting and batting, he declared it perfect.

My mother, on the other hand, was about to go way overboard. She wanted to put a doll inside the bump.

"That's just wrong," Jorge said. "Too creepy."

I agreed. But she thought it would add to the realism. She even suggested putting a moving doll in there, something that would crawl around on me all day, so that I would squirm and talk about the baby kicking.

"Okay, Mom, now you're just going too far," I said. I'm surprised she didn't try to install something with a heartbeat sound effect.

Right after spring break, I thought, was the perfect time for my new bump's grand entrance. It meant that people hadn't seen me in more than a week, so they might think the growth had been more gradual than it was. I wore a shirt that was fitted and showed off the bump, and walked into class.

I felt like a zoo animal.

All eyes went straight to my belly before people looked at my face. The whispers and judgmental looks were amplified. It was like this protrusion around my midsection was a scarlet letter, a badge of shame that showed I was marked for a life of failure and misery because I had sinned. I'd had sex. As if none of them had.

It occurred to me that I'd never really know how many of my classmates had been pregnant. Fifteen to 20 percent of all pregnancies end in miscarriages, and 45 percent of teens who get pregnant have abortions. Then there are the ones who just drop out without telling anyone why, or move to a different school. And it's not as if those walking the halls with baby bumps are the only ones who've shown bad judgment—but we're the easiest targets.

Sitting down at my desk in each classroom was a challenge, navigating how to slide into my chair with my belly. But once seated, at least I didn't feel the same level of anxiety that I did when I walked through the halls between classes or into the lunchroom. I had no idea I was going to attract this much attention, and it made me feel miserable.

I'd see a group of girls purposely not making eye contact with me, just shaking their heads and gossiping with each other as I came near. My urge was to go up to them and say, "What's so interesting? If you have something to say, say it to my face."

I never did anything like that, partly because I knew I couldn't risk blowing my project by getting into a fight in school. So I mostly just kept my head down and kept walking whenever I saw people talking about me. Did they think getting pregnant had also affected my eyesight? Did they think I couldn't see them huddling together, putting their hands over their mouths to cover whatever insults they were sharing about me?

I wanted to hide. It was exhausting to feel like people were judging me all day. I went home and cried and wished I'd never started this project.

"Mr. Greene was right. This is too hard," I said.

"It's going to be worth it," Jorge reminded me. We had to keep each other going, because the truth was that, day after day, it didn't feel worth it to either of us. Jorge continued feeling isolated from his friends because they wouldn't stop ragging on him about the pregnancy.

Several of my friends and peers made the comment, "It

was bound to happen." "I'm not surprised," one said. Really? Why were they not surprised? What had I ever done to indicate that I was irresponsible or didn't have my priorities straight? Another friend who had said encouraging things to my face was saying different things behind my back like, "Let's see what kind of mom she really is after Jorge leaves her. She's going to be a single mom with nothing, and *then* we'll see what she thinks about having a kid."

I felt backstabbed. These people knew me, knew how hard I worked to have a real future. I hated that they were talking as if they knew all along I'd end up a statistic.

"Going through the halls and walking in the classrooms, having to hear everything everyone is whispering about me, becomes harder and harder each day," I wrote in my journal. "I want to tell everyone to leave me alone."

When I came home, I might or might not be able to take off the bump, depending on who was around. My mom and I were the only people who lived there, so I was free to take it off when it was just us, but if any of my older nieces and nephews were there, I couldn't. My grandmother's mind wasn't clear enough to understand any of it, so I never had to explain things to her. I didn't tell her I was pregnant, nor did I have to reveal later that I really wasn't. I also didn't have to tell my father, since I never saw him during the time I was supposed to be pregnant.

Both before and during my project, I watched shows like

16 and Pregnant and *Teen Mom* to see what they offered. I think the people who say they glamorize teen pregnancy haven't actually watched the shows. Those shows aren't glamorous. They present the downsides of teen pregnancy, though there are not a lot of moments where I see the girls talk about what they're going through. The girls on the shows have ended up in jail, been on drugs, dealt with breakups and family problems. . . . They don't paint a picture of teen pregnancy as something fun that everyone should try.

The problem is that the media makes stars out of these girls and their boyfriends.

Why do we know every time Amber Portwood gets a piercing, or loses or gains weight, or makes up or breaks up with her boyfriend? Why are cameras following this girl around as if she's someone important for the public to know about? Why do more than 250,000 people follow Farrah Abraham on Twitter to find out the details of her boob job?

That's where the "glamour" comes in. The girls on these shows are actually on the covers of magazines, and they get stylists to do their hair and makeup, and they get to live like celebrities. Whether the attention is good or bad, it's *attention*, and it's something so many adolescents are searching for.

Lots of us feel invisible in our regular lives. When kids don't feel like they stand out for any reason, sometimes they look for ways to get noticed. So the real danger of these shows is that teens who are easily influenced may say, "If I got pregnant, I could go on a show like that and get famous. People would pay attention to me then."

It's not going to affect most teens that way—we're not as dumb as people suspect—but there's a subset of girls who will latch on and think, "These girls get paid and hang out with celebrities," and not see past that. The reality is that Amber Portwood was suicidal and may lose custody of her child because she can't get her act together. Did the media spotlight push her over the edge, or would she have ended up the same no matter what? No idea, but it doesn't seem responsible for the paparazzi to continue following these girls around when their emotional states are so messed up. How are their children going to feel in a few years when their friends in school know all about their parents' personal lives, and their parents' bad behaviors are archived forever on DVDs and the Internet?

Similarly, look at what happened with Jamie Lynn Spears. Sure, she had a show on Nickelodeon, but to the average person, she was no one but Britney Spears's younger sister until she got pregnant. It must have been hard living in the shadow of one of the most famous pop stars on the planet. . . . Well, here was one way for her to get noticed on her own. When the baby was born, *OK!* magazine reportedly paid $1 million for the right to an interview and the first published photos, and it was the bestselling American issue they ever had.

On the cover was a photo of Jamie Lynn smiling, holding her sleeping baby, and saying, "Being a mom is the best feeling in the world." What message does that send? She has much more money and access to support than the average teen mom. Normal teens are lucky if they get to brush their hair in the morning after having a newborn baby, and they're freaking out over how they're going to pay for expenses. But does it get implanted in teens' minds that having a baby is the best feeling in the world?

For some, yes, it does.

A fifteen-year-old girl on a message board wrote asking for advice — she had been watching *Teen Mom* and decided she wanted to have a baby. She wanted to know if people thought that was crazy. Another fifteen-year-old wrote back to say that she had been having the same thoughts a few months earlier, until she really thought through the consequences. "I honestly thought that having a baby would be so cute and you would always be able to have someone at your side who always loved you and you could unconditionally love without being hurt. I was lacking that relationship in my life and I think it was something that I craved . . . I wanted a little girl that I could dress up in cute little clothes."

And who was going to pay for those cute clothes? And what about when her baby pooped on her cute clothes for the eighth time that day and no one was there to help do laundry or give her a break to take a nap? What about when the baby cried for two hours straight every day for a month, and nothing worked to soothe her, and she couldn't just walk away or turn it off? I wished I could send a message to the teens with that romanticized view of motherhood: "Spend a week with me and my family, and then let me know if you still think teen pregnancy sounds like fun."

Just trailing me for a day might have given them a different impression, and I wasn't even really pregnant. Having people give you "that look" everywhere you go is enough to make pregnancy a demoralizing experience. Then there's the fact that you can't do what everyone else does anymore, like staying out late and eating junk food and playing sports and just being a regular teen. It's such an isolating experience even before the baby arrives.

In February and March, I went a couple of times to visit the college I was planning to attend. I took the belly off while I was there—but I was so nervous that someone else from my high school or community might be visiting. It was only an hour or so away from Toppenish, and several seniors from my class were going there in the fall. I just didn't want to make my entrance at my new college as "the pregnant girl," and then have to deal with people trying to figure out later what happened to my baby.

In school, I tried to carry myself in a way that didn't encourage people to touch my belly, but it still happened sometimes. No one questioned how real it felt.

"You're so tiny that it really shows on you," someone said. "Can I touch it?"

I smiled and nodded, even though I wished she hadn't asked.

After some time, the belly began sort of "decomposing." The wire would get misshapen and stick me in the sides, especially when I sat down. And the clay dried out and crumbled. We were constantly altering it and making minor fixes.

I couldn't really bend over, because each time I did, the side of the bump would get stuck pointing outward. Before I learned this lesson, I had bent over to pick something up and then sat at my desk, unaware that the wire was pushing out wrong on my side. Alex, a friend of mine, reached over to touch it before I could object. He said, "Oh, wow! Is that a foot?"

"Yes," I agreed, somehow managing not to laugh.

"That's so cool!"

I quietly adjusted it when he wasn't looking.

Wearing the bump made me feel so conspicuous. Even my teachers noticed the way that students were making side comments about me and leaving me out of conversations. Saida took it personally when people said negative things about me, and I once had to really calm her down when she wanted to go after someone who had insulted me and said I was becoming "annoying" now that I was pregnant.

"Saida, it's okay. It's not real," I said. "Just write it all down. I'm doing this for a purpose."

I had to keep reminding myself of the same thing, because there were days—many of them—that I just wanted to quit and be myself again.

Sonya knew this, so when we were with the family, she'd cheerily ask, "How's the pregnancy going?"

"Shut up," I muttered.

I should have learned to crochet instead.

Since I wasn't able to go through the normal channels to get my real project approved, I also had to work on a second senior project as a decoy, so no one would question why I hadn't submitted a senior project application and why I wasn't attending meetings with my adviser. For my decoy project, I wanted to job-shadow a social worker, which the Senior Boards committee approved. Luckily Mrs. Straehle knew someone who worked with the school, so I didn't have to work hard to find my mentor.

Julie Valdez worked with foster care students in our district, and at a local safe haven after-school program that gave kids a place to go to use computers and play sports and hang out, with the hopes of reducing gang violence, drugs, and other youth crime. I went there to meet her, and we talked about what it was like to be a social worker.

There were so many cases she told me about that were heartbreaking. Kids with no stability in their lives and no parents to call their own, just moved from house to house with no one who really loved them or was committed to them. No one to take them to the movies or buy them new clothes, no one who really cared the way parents are supposed to care.

"You have to be very strong-hearted to do this kind of work," she told me. "It's not easy. You'll see a lot of very bad situations and your heart will go out to them, but you can't get too attached to each case, because they come and go. Foster kids move to different districts, and you won't see them anymore."

She also dealt with many teen moms, and had seen first-hand how often parents would kick the girls out and leave them to fend for themselves. Sometimes the girl would move in with the boyfriend, who usually didn't have anything either, and they'd have to figure out how to make ends meet without parents to support or guide them. The social worker was there, in part, to make sure that the mother and baby had the basics they needed—a crib, diapers, wipes, and so on. And there, too, the social worker's role would usually end. She couldn't get too attached to the teen moms because they'd soon be gone, too, with just the hope that they'd learn to navigate the rest of parenthood well.

I explained to her the real situation about my pregnancy project. She offered to come to school to "check on me" to make my pregnancy more realistic.

"Whenever girls in school get pregnant, a social worker comes to check on them," she explained.

I told her that wasn't necessary, but it was so nice of her to offer. She was already taking so much time out of her schedule to mentor me. It solidified my career goal of going into foster care work because I could see how much was needed, and how many kids could be helped with the right role models.

This was the project I would talk about when I went to advisory group meetings with other people from my class. We'd get together to talk about our progress, help each other get our portfolios and presentations ready, and make sure we were on track with the requirements for graduation. One of the guys in my group was someone I'd met back in grade school, but I still didn't know him well. I liked him, though — always thought he was smart, even though I don't think he knew that about himself. During our junior year, I saw him writing something, and it triggered a funny memory.

"You still have the same handwriting from the third grade," I said.

"You remember what my *third grade* handwriting looked like?" he asked.

I laughed. "I guess I don't know that many people. I remember stuff like that."

That started our first real conversation and our friendship. He was an athlete who did only as well as he needed to in school so he wouldn't get kicked off his sports teams; you couldn't stay in sports if you had failing grades. He would get

Bs and Cs and think that was fine. I knew he could do better than that, and I told him so.

"I see so much potential in you beyond sports. You would do really well in college if you just take school a little more seriously."

I tried to help him get his portfolio together, and I would encourage him to study and bring his grades up. He and another friend in the advisory group started calling me "Mom." I asked him why, and he said, "Because you're like she is—you keep me in check, and I appreciate that."

One day before class he came running over to me, beaming like a flashlight.

"Lookit, lookit, look, look, look!" he yelled.

"What?" I said.

He thrust a piece of paper at me. It was his report card.

"I have all As! Are you proud of me?"

I grinned. "Why do you care if I'm proud of you?"

"Because you're the one who pushed me the most. I got these grades so you could be proud and see that I'm starting to do better."

"That's awesome. I knew you could do it, and you should be proud of *yourself*."

It was cute how excited he was, and it felt really good to know I could have that kind of impact on somebody just by believing in him and encouraging him. It made me think about what I hoped to achieve with my project. Would people get it? Would it make the kind of difference I hoped?

It's worth it if one person thinks twice and takes responsibility for her body and doesn't wind up pregnant because of it. It's worth it if one person realizes he doesn't have to believe the stereotypes that other people have about him, and that he can exceed everyone's expectations.

I thought about people who had risen above what was expected of them, and how they changed the world by beating the odds. Helen Keller, whose own parents never expected her to do much of anything because of her disabilities—but she had that one person to push her and believe in her. Rosa Parks, who refused to believe that she was a second-class citizen because of her skin color. Stevie Wonder, Andrea Bocelli, and Ray Charles, who all found their place in the music world despite being blind. Babe Ruth, parentless at age seven when his parents handed him over to Catholic missionaries.

I didn't expect my life to be as grand as any of theirs, but you just never know who walks among you. The kid sitting next to you in class could be the one who finds the cure for cancer, or solves our environmental crisis . . . as long as he doesn't get discouraged along the way and quit. That's what I started thinking about in terms of my project. I wondered if I could present my work in such a way that it would inspire people to believe in themselves and achieve more.

My own frustrations were wearing me out, though. It was

getting harder to know who I could trust, and overall, I was just getting a lot more negative attention than I'd bargained for. Maybe people were more apt to gossip about me because I was a good student and someone who didn't go out drinking and sleeping around—maybe it was more scandalous. Or maybe all the girls who had gotten pregnant in our high school went through this, and I just didn't realize how bad it was.

Why do teens like to gossip so much? Why do we get into each other's business and pick apart the weak spots, instead of talking about each other's best qualities and achievements? Enough of us have been on the receiving end of malicious gossip to understand how hurtful it is, and yet we do it anyway, without even giving it a second thought. . . . "Hey, did you hear about So-and-So?" Instead of leaning in, we should be butting out.

Adding to my frustration, my activities had to be limited. I wanted to join my friends in the leadership group when they volunteered to help build a Habitat for Humanity house, but Mrs. Dorr told me I should wait for a more suitable project. They didn't want a pregnant girl on a construction site swinging a hammer around.

There was one morning in March before school that I'm not proud of, when I snapped at my mom. My fake belly was not behaving anymore, and she was trying and trying to fix it so the wires wouldn't stick into me and the clay would stay put, but I was running late to class and had to go.

"Just leave it!" I yelled. "Forget it!"

Then I got into an argument with Jorge, and I just got mad at God for letting this be so hard.

"Where are you?" I prayed. "I don't want to go through this anymore. You're supposed to ease my burdens when it's too much to take. Well, it's too much to take now! I'm tired of feeling like this."

I felt myself sinking into depression and questioning my faith. April couldn't come fast enough. The lower I sank, the more I feared that there wouldn't be a point to any of it. When I started the project, I was so sure I would be able to make a difference, but now I worried that I was going through this suffering for nothing but my own experience. Sure, now I'd understand teen moms better, but that was supposed to be only one part of my project; the rest was to communicate something with the other kids in my school. Right then, I felt like most of them were too busy making me into a joke to learn anything from me.

"How are you doing?" one girl asked me. She was a teen mom in my school who had already had her baby. We had never really talked before, but now she felt a kinship with me. "You have to really brace yourself for what's to come. I know how hard it is, and how hard it is to walk around school like this. You get a lot of put-downs from people, right?"

"Yeah," I said. "I guess I knew I would, but it's hard to deal with it every day."

"I know what you mean. Family, friends, everybody. The people who you think are going to be there for you aren't there for you, and you wind up just having to get stronger and stronger within yourself, because it's not going to get easier. The baby comes and then you have all new things to deal with besides just what people say about you."

She told me about how hard it was for her to be in school, trying to coordinate a schedule with babysitters and work, and trying to pay for rent and diapers at the same time. I had seen the same things in my family, but it was touching for this girl to be willing to share her story with me. I hated that she was going through it for real and would one day find out that I was just pretending. I didn't have the back pain I said I had, and I didn't have to wake up six times a night to go to the bathroom or change positions. I could go home and take the bump off, stretch and touch my toes and eat whatever I wanted. Mostly, I didn't have to figure out how in the world I was going to stay emotionally and financially stable and secure a future for both myself and a child.

Talking to her, and to other teen moms who opened up to me about their struggles, helped me put things in perspective.

Every time I heard about friends hooking up at a party or messing around with each other casually, I wanted to say, *You do not want to go through this.* People just don't think about the consequences when they're in the moment, because it's a drag. But those few seconds, when one of them needs to stop and think before acting on impulse — those are the seconds that could save them both from a really hard life.

Maybe it's not easy and maybe it's not cool to be the one to say, "I'm not ready for this," or at least, "Let's stop and use protection." But being a seventeen-year-old mom is not cool, either. Everyone oohs and ahhs over your baby for five minutes, and then you get left in the dust to deal with your responsibilities while your friends are still out there being kids.

And all those big dreams you had about being a teacher or a doctor or owning a business, the fantasies about the places you'd travel, and the way you'd meet the right person and get married and have kids together and a dog and a pool . . . those dreams get harder and harder to reach.

It was sad talking to these young moms about how hard their lives were, and I felt so frustrated for them. None of them sounded happy. They were all struggling, and probably would be for a very long time. My mom has never stopped struggling. I have to wonder what her life might have been like if she had just stopped and said, "I'm not ready" back when she was fourteen. Of course she says she doesn't regret her kids, but she wishes she had waited to have them.

Her own dreams keep getting pushed back to "someday" because now she has to help with the grandkids. I often fantasized about how I could help her have time to do something for herself—go back and get her GED, or travel, or take up a hobby just for fun. I'm not sure if she even knows what her interests are anymore; she's been responsible for everyone else since she was a kid herself. I thought about becoming a psychologist or social worker and how that might change not only my life but hers, too.

For now, both of us and Jorge were just waiting for the day when I could go back to being me again. No more lies and no more bump. I just wanted to be able to walk into a classroom with my head held high again, in a regular pair of jeans, with nobody staring and whispering. I wanted my old sanctuary back. Jorge wanted his family and friends to get off his back, and my mom wanted to stop lying to my brothers and sisters.

"This needs to be over," she said to me.

"Soon, Mom," I said.

Our English class was taking a trip to Ashland, Oregon, for the Shakespeare Festival, and that was my light at the end of the tunnel. I knew I was going to do my presentation two days before that, and then go on the trip as my unpregnant self. What a relief it was going to be to toss that darn "baby bump" in the garbage. I never wanted to see it again.

CHAPTER 10

THE BIG REVEAL

No one had ever presented their School Boards speech in front of the whole school before, but Mr. Greene and I thought it would have the most impact if everyone heard my message straight from me. I had planned from the start to give my presentation to everyone, but I thought I would have to do it in groups for each grade. Instead, we realized, it was going to lose a lot of steam if one grade found out first and then left the assembly saying, "Hey, guess what?" to their friends in other grades.

So Mr. Greene scheduled a time when the entire student body would come to the gymnasium for my speech. Before my big reveal, Mr. Greene wanted me to tell the teachers. I didn't want to; I was hoping to reveal it to everyone at once, with the exception of just a few people who I thought should be prepared ahead of time.

Of course, Mr. Myers was at the top of my list. I couldn't wait to get this off my chest and tell him the truth, so Mr. Greene invited him and two other teachers to come to his office with me two days before the assembly, right after I'd done the dress rehearsal of my presentation.

"There's something I need to tell you," I started. As nervous as I had been when I first announced I was pregnant, now I was even *more* nervous. "My senior project is about stereotypes, rumors, and statistics, and in order to study my topic, I introduced a fake pregnancy so I could learn about people's reactions. I wanted to tell you before I tell the rest of the school."

No one really said anything, so I kept nervously talking until Mr. Myers finally leaned in and said, "Are you serious?"

"Yes."

He didn't look happy. He looked sort of flustered and mad.

After several seconds, he said, "The scientist in me thinks you ran a great experiment and you had to control your variables, but the human in me feels lied to."

The other two teachers just seemed relieved and didn't say much, but Mr. Myers paced around and said that he felt his trust was betrayed. After a while, Mr. Greene took him aside and asked if he was okay, and I was left feeling pretty lousy again. It wasn't the sense of relief I had hoped for.

The night before the assembly, I cried and cried. I was

very worried about how people would take it, especially after I saw Mr. Myers's reaction. If he felt so betrayed, how were our families and close friends going to feel? Was I going to have any friends left at the end of this, aside from Saida?

Jorge was with me that night, and he held me. "It's going to be okay. People will understand."

"I'm so scared. What if everybody hates me?"

"Nobody is going to hate you."

He kept trying to reassure me, but I still got very little sleep that night. I just hadn't expected a reaction like Mr. Myers's. I don't know exactly what I expected, but not that. He was one of the ones I counted on to be proud of me for doing something this big. Now I was more worried than ever that people weren't going to understand why I did this, or that they were going to be angry to have been deceived, regardless of the intent.

I went to school the next day with a bad case of panic. I had done some speaking in front of classes before, but never anything on this scale, and certainly never anything this nerve-racking. With my permission, my mentor had called the local paper to tell them I was going to do a good presentation about stereotypes and rumors, and they offered to send a reporter. That barely registered on my nervousness scale; I was so freaked out about doing the presentation in front of my peers and teachers that the reporter was just one more body in the stands.

Before the assembly, the reporter from the *Yakima Herald-Republic*, Adriana Janovich, did briefly talk to me and let me know that she'd try to write up a "little article" that would go somewhere in the paper. She didn't know what the presentation was going to be about, but I pictured the article being somewhere between the notes about church yard sales and the tips for storing vegetables longer in the refrigerator.

The superintendent, Mr. Cerna, had been at a conference, and he left the other side of the state at five thirty a.m. just to make it back in time for my ten-fifteen presentation. "I wouldn't miss it for the world," he said.

The pressure was mounting. I hoped I would make it worthwhile for Mr. Cerna and for everyone else. I thought about how I was dragging Saida into the same sort of possible backlash that I might receive, so I talked to her that morning.

"If you don't want people to know that you knew all along, I will tell them I just told you a few days ago. If you don't want our friends thinking they can't trust you, I can pretend you didn't know."

"No, I've gone this far with you already; I'm going all the way," she said. "I'll stand up with you and face it. And if everyone hates us, well, at least school is over in a month."

In the hallway just before my presentation, a student I'd never spoken to before said, "So this assembly is for your senior project?"

I nodded.

"What's it about?"

"Character education and a couple of other things."

"Sounds pretty boring."

"Believe me, it won't be boring."

My mom came to school that day to watch my presentation, and she brought my oldest niece — the one who's actually a year older than me. Nievitas couldn't make it, but my mom told her daughter that I was going to receive an award at school. Sonya was there, and so was Jorge. One of my teachers was sitting behind Jorge at the assembly and said to him before I began, "How far along is Gaby?"

He had forgotten how far along I was supposed to be, so he just muttered, "It won't be long now."

That was the truth! I watched the teachers and eight hundred students file into the gymnasium and sit in the stands. My hands shook as I clutched my pile of index cards, notes that would keep my speech on track. Behind me was the projector screen I would use to show my PowerPoint presentation and video clips. I had put it together at home so I wouldn't get caught at school, and I'd been able to practice only once, when Mr. Greene had closed off the gym doors so I could do a run-through.

There would be about seven girls in the audience who really were pregnant, and I worried about their reactions especially. I hoped they would know I wasn't trying to embarrass them or betray their trust, but that I was honestly trying to help give them a voice.

A good friend of mine named Emmanuel introduced me. "Think of somebody in your life who you consider courageous and amazing . . . maybe you can think of a couple of people. Who I'm presenting today is a really close friend of mine, and when I think of somebody courageous and amazing, Gaby's one of the people I think of."

I sure hoped he'd still think so in about fifteen minutes. He didn't know what my project was actually about.

Now it was my turn. I held the microphone and faced the crowd. "My name is Gaby Rodriguez. I'm seventeen years old and a soon-to-be teen mom, and I became a statistic," I started. "In reality, everybody is a statistic, but I moved from the percentage of teens who aren't pregnant to the percentage who are. There are many statistics out there, such as the ones shown on the screen—like, annually, a quarter of a million births are to unmarried teen moms; one in four sexually active teens become infected with an STD; and 92.9 percent of Caucasians graduate, compared to 86.9 percent of African Americans and only 61.8 percent of Latinos. My purpose today is to tell you about my experience as a soon-to-be teen mom and the stereotypes and rumors that came along with that."

Then I showed a short video I found on YouTube called "Stop Stereotypes. Now." It showed pictures of children being excluded and whispered about, along with a few sentences on the possible consequences of stereotypes and rumors—depression, stress, drugs, violence, and even death. Putting on the video gave me a minute to breathe and mentally prepare myself for the next section.

"Throughout life, we are put into boxes to categorize how people see and know us. This is how stereotypes originate, because people would rather read the labels on the box instead of taking a look and seeing what's inside. . . . People began to stereotype me as a pregnant teen who is irresponsible, going to get my way because they thought people were going to be nicer to me because of the baby, not willing to continue in school, and even, 'Oh, I knew she was going to get pregnant. It was bound to happen anyway.' Not many people are willing to talk about being on the receiving end, but here I am today to let you know, being your peer and walking in the same halls as you do, that I hear what's being said, and I know you would rather talk about the stereotypes at hand than the stereotypes being broken."

My second video was a public service announcement made by students in a media class. It showed kids holding up large signs with negative stereotypes about teens written on them: that we're party animals, we're bad drivers, we make bad decisions, we are self-centered, and so on. Each person dropped their sign to show another sign behind it with statements that went against the stereotype: "I'm a member of Big

Brothers of America," "I'm a straight-A student," and similar messages.

"As for the situation I'm in, many things were said about me. Many things traveled all the way back to me."

Then came the first really hard part—exposing the individual comments people had made, which I knew would embarrass the people who'd made them, even if I didn't identify them personally. I had given several students and teachers index cards containing some of these comments. One by one, people read them.

"She isn't even taking her pregnancy seriously. She needs to take responsibility and grow up."

"She's so dumb. Doesn't she know she just ruined her life?"

"Her attitude is changing, and it might be because of the baby, or she was always this annoying and I never realized it."

"Some say she will make a good mom, but I think that will change after the baby is here."

"I think her boyfriend will bail, and then she'll see what a big mistake she made."

"Her family won't make a big deal out of this because they're used to teen moms."

I continued with my speech. "Most of you don't realize that any time you do or say something, there's always someone watching—siblings, other family members, or friends. That is why you have to set an example."

I told them about Genaro and how he was stereotyped because his father was an alcoholic. "He began to use and abuse alcohol. Now he has his own little girls, and hopefully he will set a good example."

The next video I showed was a commercial from the National Association for Prevention of Child Abuse and Neglect in Australia, and I really encourage you to check it out on YouTube by searching for "Children See, Children Do." It's a powerful video depicting children imitating their parents or other adults: smoking, displaying road rage, being racist, and perpetuating domestic violence.

"I grew up in a pretty big family, and I've seen a lot of different things. I have four brothers and three sisters who were always telling me I would end up like my older sister, because she's who I spent most of my time with. They constantly told me how I was going to get pregnant at an early age, drop out of school, and not continue to college. My whole life I had to fight against the stereotypes and the labels they gave me. To this day, I continue to fight *not* to live my life as a stereotype and the hot topic of everyone's rumors. You're probably wondering, How is this seventeen-year-old fighting against stereotypes and rumors when it seems that she did the complete opposite?"

It was time for the big finale, and I could hardly breathe.

"I'm fighting against those stereotypes and rumors because the reality is . . . I'm not pregnant."

I reached down to remove my fake belly. I hadn't fully attached it with the belly band the way I normally did in school; to make it easier to remove, I had just zipped it into my sweatshirt and kept it pressed against my body with one arm. Even so, it took a minute to maneuver out, and during that time, first there was silence, then a loud "Whaaaaaat?" and some gasps and laughs.

"That's awesome!" someone called out.

Once I finished removing it, the room burst into applause, and I couldn't hold back the tears.

"As you can see, this project was very difficult for me," I said. It was hard to finish the speech. Emotion overcame me: relief, happiness, fear. All the weight was lifted now, but I still had no idea what the fallout would be. As I stumbled over my next words because I couldn't speak through the tears, a student called out, "You go, Gaby. You've got this."

It was phenomenal to feel that wave of support. There were a number of people in the audience crying now, too. One of my closest friends was among them, and I'd later learn that she was having trouble catching her breath and felt really overwhelmed to realize that all of our conversations on the subject had been fake.

I apologized to everyone who was affected by my project, saying that I had no intention of hurting anyone and hoped people wouldn't take it personally. Then I talked about what I hoped they would take away from my presentation.

157

"Every single one of you has the power to go to college and graduate, and I challenge each of you to take this as an example. You have to fight for what you want in life. You can't live your life under a stereotype. You can't live your life in the shadow of your brothers or sisters or parents; you have to live *your* life, and make it a good life, because you only have one."

I took many questions from the audience after my speech, and to start, they mostly wanted to know whether I ever felt like quitting the project, whether my family knew about it, and what my real plans were for college. Then my friend Alex stood up and asked, "Do you know how dumb you made people feel when they thought they felt a heartbeat or a foot?"

This time I couldn't help but laugh a little. Alex was the one who thought he had felt a foot.

"I do know how dumb I made people feel, and I'm sorry, Alex. When I would sit down, the belly would bend out the sides, so what you felt was a bump, but it wasn't the baby. I'm sorry."

I also called out an apology to Jorge's sister, who was in the audience and was in tears. Then one of the students lightened the mood when he joked, "Remember all those times we gave you our lunches because we thought you were pregnant? How does that make you feel?"

It made it easier for me to relax as I saw that other people were able to, also. As my time came to a close, I asked people to contact me in person or on Facebook if they wanted to talk more, and I concluded, "I challenge you to live how you want to live and not how anyone else wants you to live."

I got a standing ovation for my presentation—the first one Mr. Greene said he'd ever seen for a student presentation. It felt amazing. After the assembly was over, so many people came over to me to tell me how moved they were and how brave they thought I was. Lots of them were students I barely knew, yet they thought enough of what I'd done to come over and congratulate me.

In the midst of everything, I looked at my mom and she looked at me, and we both started crying again. No words needed to be spoken. We just hugged and cried out of relief and joy. My mom and Jorge were so proud of me, and also so glad it was over now. No more secrets needed to be kept; it was all out in the open, and we just had to fill in our family members who couldn't be there.

Jorge turned back to the teacher who'd asked how far along I was, and the two of them laughed. "Sorry," Jorge said. "I couldn't remember how far along she was supposed to be."

Blanca, who was sitting next to Saida, couldn't stop crying, and she wondered how Saida could be so calm about it.

"Well . . . ," Saida said. "I knew."

"WHAT? You knew all along?"

Saida nodded, and Blanca punched her in the arm.

"I'm sorry. I didn't do it to lie to anyone. I just did it to help my friend."

Later our friend Nestor went up to Saida and asked, "You knew?" When Saida said yes, Nestor punched her, too.

"Okay, I guess I'm going to get hit a lot," she said.

After the assembly, the newspaper reporter wanted to go to the principal's office to interview me and some of the people involved. After making sure I had permission to miss my next class, I gladly stayed to speak with her. She kept saying, "This is going to be big. This is going to be big." I just thought she meant it was going to get a big reaction in the newspaper, which was flattering. I hoped that she'd get my message across well in the article. I knew she was also going to interview my mom, Jorge, and some of my teachers.

The rest of the day was like walking on air—so many people congratulating me, and telling me that they were touched by my project and thought I was very brave. I heard only one negative comment that day, and it was from the guy who had told me before the assembly that my project sounded boring. It turns out that after the assembly, he went around telling people, "I knew that bitch wasn't pregnant. That girl's a fucking liar!" I'd never spoken to him before that day, but he worked hard to get people riled up—he succeeded in getting the whole baseball team mad at me. It confused me why someone would be so angry when he didn't even have any contact with me. He wasn't affected by my false pregnancy in any way, so why all the venom?

I was able to brush that off because it was such a small part of what felt to me like a wonderful day. My friends were quickly forgiving and congratulated me on my presentation. One was more hurt than the others, but I talked to her about it and did my best to explain that I didn't mean to slight anyone who wasn't in on the secret; it didn't mean I didn't trust her or I thought she had a big mouth or anything like that. I explained that Saida was the only friend I told, and that was because I needed someone to report the reactions at school.

I didn't know that there were other things going on "behind the scenes" after my presentation. It turned out that several teachers were mad at Mr. Greene for approving my project and hiding it from them. One of the teachers seemed to lead her class in an unstructured gripe session about me that day, which I knew nothing about until Mr. Greene mentioned it weeks later.

Mr. Greene ended up having to call a meeting where the teachers could vent to him.

"My students were talking, and they want to fake a suicide next year," one teacher said.

"You know that, by law, you'd have to report any suicide threat to the police," another teacher said, which sort of shut her up.

"I'm asking you to present a balanced argument to your

classes," Mr. Greene said. He asked them to consider that many people had been positively touched by the experiment, and he said he didn't want people to gang up on me.

I knew there was a possibility some teachers would be upset that I didn't go through the regular channels to get my project approved, and that things could have gone wrong throughout the project. But since none of those things actually happened, I still don't understand why some of them were as angry as they were—except that nobody likes to feel duped. Maybe some of them were forced to think about the comments they had made about me or the girls who really were pregnant, and they didn't like what they had to face.

Blissfully unaware of this at the time, I went home that afternoon and celebrated the end of my "pregnancy." I turned to Jorge and said, "I'm free! I get to be me!"

"Let's just hope everything is still good tomorrow," he said. We knew that there would be some repercussions— Jorge's sister was mad at us, for one thing—but we both felt confident that anyone who was upset that day would come around once they had some time to process it and realize that it had all been for a good purpose.

Jorge's parents were confused at first when he told them.

"What do you mean she wasn't pregnant? What, did she just take off her belly?"

"Well, actually . . . she did," he said.

We spoke to both of them about my reasons for doing the

project, and I apologized for causing them any stress. They didn't seem to understand, but they said, "Well, we're glad your life won't be so hard. Now you can both go to college and do things the right way."

I made calls to all my siblings but didn't get through to everyone. Tony and Fabian were always hard to reach, but I didn't see them very often, so I figured it wouldn't be a big deal if I caught up with them in another day or two. My sisters, Javier, and Genaro were each very relieved to find out I wasn't really pregnant. Sonya's husband refused to believe her when she told him the story. He was positive that I'd had an abortion and just made up the whole senior project as a way to cover it up. It took some convincing to make him see just how far in advance I'd planned the whole thing and that Sonya had known all along.

It was the first night in a long time that I went to bed without a ton of worry on my mind. No matter what, it was over now.

At least, that's what I thought. I had no idea what awaited me the next morning.

PART 3
POSTPARTUM IMPRESSION

CHAPTER 11

THE AFTERMATH

When I got to school the next morning, I headed straight to Mr. Greene's office to find out if they'd gotten a copy of the *Yakima Herald-Republic* yet. I was hoping to read the article about me. When I approached, Mr. Greene wordlessly held up the newspaper . . . and there I was on the front cover, with the headline PREGNOT.

"The front cover!" I said. "But that's for really big stories. Oh my . . ."

I took the newspaper from his hands and read through the article. It was good. It was just shocking for me to feel so on display to the public all of a sudden. I was sort of freaked out, but happy to have made that kind of impact. Mr. Greene congratulated me, and I went on to class.

Little did I realize that, because the *Yakima Herald-*

Republic shares its articles with the Associated Press, my story was being transmitted through wire services to newspapers across the country. Around eight thirty that morning, I was called back to the principal's office.

"I've been getting phone calls all morning from the local news stations," he said. "They want to interview you for this evening's news. What do you think?"

I thought it was funny. I hadn't prepared for anything beyond the presentation, and it felt awkward being suddenly so exposed. In the media, you just never know how things are going to get spun or edited. Still, I'd given brief interviews for local news stations before during community events and a school engineering program, so I knew it wasn't a big deal.

I decided to go ahead and do my best because, after all, my project was for the whole community. Teen pregnancy is such an epidemic in our area that I felt good about sharing my story with people outside of my high school. Maybe I could reach more teens by doing these interviews.

I thought about some of the things I learned from the project and what I might be able to pass along. For one thing, I wanted to show people what societal opinions teen moms are up against, and how those opinions can shape a young woman's life just as much as the pregnancy itself. I hoped that I could encourage people to break the bad cycle that had become apparent to me:

A teen gets pregnant. People treat her like a pariah, so

she becomes depressed. Her boyfriend is scared off because society tells him he's in for a terrible life. She drops out of school and can't find a good job, so she ends up on welfare. She's not emotionally or financially prepared to be a parent and doesn't have a lot of support, so she's not the best mom she can be, and the baby grows up without a steady father figure. The child is 50 percent more likely to repeat a grade than his or her peers, and performs worse on standardized tests. If he's a boy, he's more likely to go to prison, and if she's a girl, she's likely to become a teen mom herself and start the cycle over again.

But I also learned that having *one person* who believes in you can make all the difference. I wanted to encourage people to become that one person in others' lives—especially to teen moms and other young people who were vulnerable or at risk.

Could I say all that on television and have it come out right?

"Do they have to interview me during school?" I asked.

"Apparently so, because they need time to edit the footage before the five o'clock news. They want your mom and Jorge, too, and they want you to wear the belly."

"Oh, great, I have to wear that thing again."

"Yep, one more day."

I thought about it. "Look, you know me, Mr. Greene. My heart and soul is in my schoolwork, and I already missed classes to get ready for the presentation and do the interview yesterday. Can I just do one interview that they all tape together?"

"No, they're competing with one another, so they want to bring their own crews and ask you their own questions. But I'll tell them to make it short."

We agreed to do it at eleven o'clock, when my lunch started, but I knew it would probably run into my next class. I spoke with that teacher, who assured me it was fine and I wouldn't miss much, so I went ahead and called my mom and Jorge to come to school. When they arrived, Mr. Greene mentioned that now there was a fourth network coming in, all the way from Seattle.

Considering how the rest of the day went, I think I'll just refer to the local networks by the order in which I did the interviews: Networks 1, 2, and 3, plus the Seattle network.

We taped a bunch of visual shots first, before the interviews. All four networks wanted to see me put the belly on and take the belly off, and then get Jorge touching the belly, me walking around the halls with the belly, and whatnot. They also wanted close-ups of the belly itself, where the reporters would sort of "dissect" what it was made of and show the different layers.

I kept saying the belly was delicate and that it couldn't take so much handling, but even so, the side of it started to crack. All those months I'd managed to keep it together, and within twenty minutes, these reporters had manhandled it enough to break it. I felt so frustrated.

Then began the sit-down interviews, which we did in two different rooms. Network 1 was no big deal. The reporter asked each of us some questions—not too long. I was able to move along to Network 2 pretty quickly, where they asked similar questions. Meeting with Network 3, however, is when things got *interesting*.

"We need to have the belly next to you on the table so viewers can see it while you're talking," said the reporter.

"Okay," I said, looking around. "Wait, where is the belly?"

"I don't know," she said. "Where did you have it last?"

"I brought it right back here to the principal's office."

I checked with the secretaries. "Have you seen a lady with a camera with my belly?"

"Oh, she's down by the cafeteria," one of them said.

It turned out that the lady from Network 1 had taken my belly and was across the building, trying it on herself and taking shots with it. I tracked her down and asked for it back.

"Hold on, let me just take a couple shots with it," she said.

I went back to tell Network 3 what was going on, and the reporter got upset. "She's trying to keep it for herself. She's hijacking the belly."

Yes, *hijacking the belly*. Was there going to be a reporter fight?

I got the belly back and started interview three, and while I was doing that, the reporter from Seattle showed up. Right away there seemed to be a weird tension between them. Then Reporter 3 kept me for a very long time to make sure she got all my best quotes before the Seattle reporter could get any.

When Network 1 realized that Network 3 was doing a much longer interview with me than they had, they tried to get me back for a few more questions. Then Network 2 found out their camera guy had a technical problem with the video and the interview hadn't actually recorded.

"I'm sorry, Gaby, but we need to re-record your interview," the guy said.

"No, she's mine now," said Reporter 3. "You had your time with her."

"That's kind of messed up," I said. "Why can't I just answer a few questions for him and come back?" After all, their interview had been very short, and it wouldn't take much time to redo it.

"Well, you're here with me now, and I'm just going to keep you for a little while longer," Reporter 3 said.

Then it was time for Seattle. In the middle of a shot where they asked me to sit and work on a computer, my cell phone rang. I picked it up.

"Gaby?"

"Yes?"

"Hi! This is *Good Morning America*."

I almost fell off the chair. Maybe they were expecting a bigger reaction, but I mostly sat there in stunned silence. This was a show in New York. How had they learned about me so fast? It hadn't sunk in that this was such a big story.

"We'd like to send a film crew out to interview you, and we can be there first thing in the morning."

"Can you hold on, please?"

I had no idea what to say, so I handed the phone to Mr. Greene.

"Who is it?" Mr. Greene asked.

"*Good Morning America*."

"How did they get your cell phone number?"

"I have no idea."

"Oh!" said the Seattle reporter. "It's *Good Morning America*? Great! Put me on the phone. I'll talk to them. Tell them that they can get the interview. We can get it done."

Did she have some kind of affiliation with them? Had she told them about me? Everything started to feel so unreal.

Even though the Seattle reporter was being pushy, Mr. Greene said he would handle it. He talked to the *Good Morning America* producer, who wanted to have a film crew interview me at three a.m. the following day—the same day I was leaving at six a.m. for our field trip to the Shakespeare Festival.

"She'll call you back," he said, and hung up. He saw my

face, which was probably pale and frozen with fear. "Gaby, come with me."

He brought Jorge and me back into his office, where I just fell apart.

"I can't handle this anymore," I said. "One reporter wants to redo the interview, the other isn't finished yet, they broke my belly, I think there's going to be a reporter turf war in the cafeteria, and *Good Morning America* wants to talk to me at *three in the morning*?"

"This is all up to you. You don't have to do any of it."

"Good, because I can't. This is just too much now. I want to go home and get ready for my trip. This is crazy."

He looked over at his window and noticed that the Seattle reporter was actually peeking through the blinds at us. He walked over and very slowly turned the blinds closed.

"You're right. This woman is scaring me," he said.

As I tried to pull myself together, Mr. Greene told me that he would help me however he could, and that I didn't need to worry about everything at once. I could take time to consider my opportunities, and handle one thing at a time after the trip.

While we talked, Jorge left to pull his car around to the back entrance of the school. Then my mom and I sneaked out, leaving Mr. Greene to explain to the reporters that I was done for the day and they'd have to make do with what they had. I'm sure they were not happy—especially Network 2, who now had nothing—but I felt like I was going to have a breakdown. It was just too much too quickly.

On my way out the back door, a student from my leadership group stopped me. She had gone to a local radio station that day to talk about a school campaign the group was doing.

"The guy at the radio station asked me to give you this," she said, handing me a business card. "He wants to schedule a time to talk to you."

Perfect timing, I thought. *That's just what I need—more media!* I took the card and drove off in Jorge's car, feeling hopeful that I could relax now. People in school knew me, and I felt protected there, but doing these interviews meant exposing my story and my feelings to strangers. Who knew how people might react? Plus, I had so many other things on my mind—the school trip was the next day and I wasn't even packed yet, I still had to prepare for my presentation to the Senior Boards committee, final exams were coming up. . . . There was too much going on for me to get distracted by the media. I just wanted my regular life back.

"I guess I can't just be me now after all," I said to Jorge.

One of Jorge's sisters was at school that day—the one who was mad at me—but once she saw how crazy things were getting and how stressed out I was, she put her own anger aside. None of us had ever imagined ending up on television about this—it just wasn't on my radar beyond the local paper, so I hadn't thought through what I might say or how to dress or how to prepare.

My phone rang and rang, even though I had stopped answering it. *Good Morning America* kept calling me from different phone numbers. I turned off my phone and my mom stopped answering hers. My principal fielded literally hundreds of phone calls from all sorts of media outlets—film producers, newspaper reporters, magazine editors, television news producers, radio hosts, bloggers, talk-show personalities. . . . The calls came from across the United States—and then even internationally. Somehow it got interpreted that I meant to be a spokeswoman for Latina teens, even though I had never intended the message to be for just one racial group or another. We all get stereotyped for different things. But that made the story even more interesting for Spanish media, so I heard from both English- *and* Spanish-language media. My Spanish is only so-so. My mom and my siblings and I never speak it at home, even though my grandmother speaks only Spanish.

I felt bad for Mr. Greene. It shouldn't have been his responsibility to field all these calls on my behalf, but I didn't know what else to do. At home, I tried to focus on how much fun the trip was going to be. A couple of hours later, my mom's cell phone rang; mine was still turned off. It was Tony.

"Gaby, what the heck is going on? I just got a call from *Good Morning America* and they are looking for you."

"*Good Morning America* called you?!"

"Yes. They were talking about your senior project about faking a pregnancy. . . . Is it true?"

"Yes."

"You're not really pregnant?"

"No. I wanted to tell you myself, but—"

"This is awesome. I'm so relieved for you. Here I was, so disappointed that you didn't learn from our mistakes, but you did. And then you did *this*. Everybody is talking about it."

"I know. How did *Good Morning America* find you when *I* can't even find you?"

"I have no idea!"

"What did you say to them?"

"Nothing! I kind of hung up on them."

It turned out that he was so flustered when they said I wasn't pregnant, he had no idea what to say, so he just hung up and started tracking me down. Meanwhile, other people called him to say, "Hey, I saw your sister in the paper."

He had to get back to work soon after that, but I next heard from Sonya, who let me know that *Good Morning America* had also called her and Javier. What's so phenomenal is that I never mentioned my siblings by name in any of my interviews, and we don't have the same last names. I have my mother's maiden name, and my siblings have either their father's last name or their husbands' last names. Yet somehow, within hours, *Good Morning America* had found the numbers of our cell phones and our house phones. I have never found out how.

"They want our comments, but mostly they're trying to get us to help them find you," Sonya said. She was at Javier's house at the time, helping Javier's wife, Kathy, with her daycare business. "We're just saying we don't know anything."

"I think that's the best idea for now," I agreed. I called the rest of my brothers and sisters and told them to do the same.

"If you get a call and it's not from the 509 area code, don't even answer."

Before I went to bed that night, I turned on my phone to check my voicemail and make sure none of my other family or friends had tried calling me. There were fourteen voicemails . . . every one of them from *Good Morning America*.

Mr. Greene advised me to go on our school trip for a few days and let this settle in, so that's what I tried to do. I left my phone back in Toppenish. On the bus, I spoke with a teacher, Ms. Andrews, whom I'd rarely spoken with before, and had a great conversation. She opened up to me about how she was trying to quit smoking and some things about her family, and I opened up to her about how scared I was of everything that was happening. She promised that if anyone tried to bother me on the trip, she'd be my personal bodyguard.

When we got into town, Saida and I headed for the Yogurt Hut, a place we absolutely love in Oregon. The whole class would hang out there—downstairs you could buy frozen yogurt, and upstairs they had air hockey and Foosball and pool and other games. As we approached, I couldn't believe what I saw. . . . No, not people dressed up in Shakespeare garb, but a car with a network television news logo on it.

Someone had followed us all the way to Ashland, Oregon.

I froze in my tracks.

Saida asked, "What's wrong?"

"Look," I said.

The car was parked right in front of the Yogurt Hut.

"Don't tell me they're here for you," she said.

"What are we supposed to do?"

We walked slowly around the corner to scope out the situation. No one was in the car, and we didn't see anyone on the street carrying a camera, so we ran into the Yogurt Hut and right upstairs. I sat near a window and stared out at the car.

"Don't worry; they don't know you're here. And they can't follow you in anyway. They won't tape inside a business."

I tried to believe her. I walked around and made myself play some games and dial down my paranoia. When we were ready to leave, I thought, *Please be gone, please be gone, please be gone.* Then we walked out the door and . . . the car was gone!

Maybe they weren't here for me after all. Maybe they were just here to do a report on the Shakespeare Festival.

We headed on toward the theater, where we were scheduled to take a class picture on the front lawn. About six of us were walking toward the meeting spot when I saw a woman shaking Ms. Andrews's hand.

"So Gaby didn't come on the trip?" she asked.

Ms. Andrews was telling the reporter that I had been feeling sick that morning and stayed home. When I realized what was going on, I could not get out of there fast enough. I turned right around and started walking back in the direction we'd come. The others turned and followed me. "What's wrong?"

"That is a freaking reporter right there," I said.

A few of them turned to look, but I kept walking. Then I heard, "Are you Gaby Rodriguez?"

Without saying anything to each other, our group all started running like crazy. Then, as if we had devised a plan in advance, some of us headed one way and others headed another way, zig-zagging around to throw off the reporters and camera crew.

I ducked into a restaurant, where my friend Francisco gave me his jacket and my friend Alma gave me her glasses. I could not believe I had to go incognito on a school field trip.

"You're going to be fine," Francisco said. "We're not going to let her get near you."

All of these students had been in my class for the last four years, and though I wasn't necessarily close with all of them, in that moment, I felt so united with them. It was a great feeling of support. When it was time to go into the theater, a few other friends distracted the reporter while I hurried inside. I knew I'd be safe there because you had to have a ticket to get in, and the show was sold out.

I thought about how many people would have loved to be in my position—so many people were chasing fame, and here I was running away from it.

While I was away, Mr. Greene was trying his best to keep up with the calls. ABC, NBC, and CBS had each sent someone to meet with him and discuss having me do my first national television interview on their network. He heard them out, and then said he'd set up a time when I got back from my trip when they could each present their pitch to me, to talk about why I should go with them first. He checked in with me through the chaperones to let me know what was happening and to make sure I was okay.

He also tried keeping a list of all the other calls he received for me. That list included, among dozens of others, *Inside Edition*, the *Dr. Drew Show*, the *Ellen Degeneres Show*, Katie Couric, *Latina* magazine, Univision, *Harper's Magazine*, the American Civil Liberties Union of Washington, Merrimack College in Massachusetts, NPR, the BBC, MSNBC New York, Reuters news agency, and HLN. On top of that were radio stations across the United States and in Ireland, Canada, and England; film producers; and book publishers.

And the story had blown up on the Internet. It seemed to be relevant in lots of different circles: pregnancy websites, mom blogs, local news discussions, ethics websites, education forums. . . . Most of the articles and comments were positive, with clever headlines and a general tone of amazement that anyone would want to do what I did. Several talked about how I "gave up" my senior year to do this, but I never felt that way. I felt I was making it more meaningful.

The comments, however, got heated at times and cruel at others. I read many of them at first, before deciding it would be healthier not to. The negativity centered around a few things:

- Misunderstanding my purpose

  "The goal is to make it more acceptable to have out of wedlock children and have the rest of us embrace it. Hmmm. No!"

"Wow! Having a baby in your teens is glamorous stuff!! Woohoo! All the girls should get knocked up, then when they become rich and famous they can get plastic surgery and liposuction to remove all the pregnancy fat!"

- Believing I was seeking fame and attention

"You're telling me that there were rumors she was irresponsible and won't go to college? My God, the horror! So much information was gained now that we know those rumors were flying around about a pregnant girl. Seriously, what was the point of this sham? Nothing was learned from it and nothing was gained. This was not a display of courage, this was a display of attention seeking."

"She was using other peoples [sic] problems to further her 15 minutes. She and the school would have been better served if she actually tried to help one of the girls in her class who was pregnant. What she did was slap every pregnant teen in the face by pulling this prank."

"What an idiot. Another attention whore. Look at me look at me look at meeeee!"

- The way it made the community look bad

   "I am embarrased [sic] that this girl is getting this much press for something that does nothing for the community except renforce [sic] that fact that in the Yakima County there is a high number of hispanic [sic] girls who get pregnant . . . She is a cruel and selfish little girl who needs to learn that her actions not only affect her but her family and ultimently [sic] her entire community."

- The deception

   "I mean COME ON who did she really help??? Only other liars to learn how to lie."

   "A childish and unimaginative stunt. Maybe in college she can write a paper about what having no friends is like because she's a liar and a manipulator."

Jorge got a kick out of all the people online who acted self-righteous about his family. People wrote things like, "So what if her boyfriend's parents took a second mortgage on their house to buy the new parents a condo or a starter home?" Uh . . . yeah, right. And, "Those poor parents who were probably excited about a grandkid and now they have to find out it was all a lie!"

"They don't even know my family," Jorge said. "They weren't excited about the baby at all! They were totally relieved when they found out it was a lie."

I think maybe a lot of people who don't live in communities like mine pictured it differently from the way it really was. Our families were not out buying baby furniture and baby clothes for us and wanting to know about sonograms and things. They were upset when they thought we were going to have a baby. I don't mean to minimize lying to them, but none of them have suffered any long-term, deep-seated emotional breakdowns over this. We're all fine.

Sometimes it was hard to read these things about myself, but mostly I just thought it was sad that people would waste so much anger judging a stranger. Most of their comments were in reaction to maybe one or two sentences from an interview with me. Did they really think they understood my character and motivations based on two sentences?

Saida was much more upset and angry about the reactions than I was. I told her to stop looking because it wasn't worth it, and I followed that same advice. Nothing good could come of reading anonymous attacks on me online.

What amazed me, though, was how much interest there

was in this story. I didn't expect it to travel outside of my community, yet it seemed like as the days went on, interest only increased. Whatever the reason, it struck a chord, and there was no escaping this crazy phenomenon. After my trip, there were twenty-two new voicemails awaiting me—some from *Good Morning America*, but many from other shows. I don't even remember anymore; I didn't return any of the calls.

On the bus ride back from the trip on Monday, the driver had to drop me off about five miles away from the school and I had to have Jorge pick me up because the media scene at school was just chaos. You would have thought they were expecting Selena Gomez's or Demi Lovato's tour bus.

Later that day, I went to visit Mrs. Straehle to thank her for her help with my project. When I got to her classroom, she handed me copies of all the articles that had appeared in our local papers about me. She'd bought extra copies of the papers and had the articles laminated for me. It was so nice of her, especially because I hadn't even read most of the articles yet. Things had just been so crazy.

While I was standing at Mrs. Straehle's desk in the back of the classroom, a girl I knew from my leadership class came up to me with tears flowing down her cheeks and thanked me for my presentation.

She was being bullied in school for no reason I could ever figure out, and had been planning to drop out because she couldn't stand the way people gossiped and talked about her. There were a bunch of rumors about her making out with different guys behind the school and sleeping around. She was such a sweet girl, and it never made sense to me why anyone would want to hurt her. In school, she always walked around with a smile. I didn't know how hard her life was until we talked about it. "My family puts me down all the time. My mom is always telling me that I'm nothing, that I'm never going anywhere in life, that I'm a loser. You taught me that I don't have to listen to that. I can do what I want to do in my life."

She was so close to giving up in her junior year, but she told me it was my project that made her decide to hang in there.

She hugged me and cried, and it was so humbling. My biggest hope had already come true. It was all worth it, just for that.

"You're so close," I said. "You can't give up now. One more year and you can be done with this and have a fresh start."

We made plans to get together to have more of an in-depth talk. I gave her my phone number and told her to find me on Facebook, and after that, I tried to check in with her to make sure she was doing okay. When you're feeling depressed, it can feel really fake when people say, "I'm here for you . . . call me when you need me." I wanted her to know I was for real.

Several other girls opened up to me like that after my project. It seemed to break down a barrier, and it allowed people to tell me about what they were struggling with. I felt honored that they would trust me and share such personal things.

Just about every day I would get called to the principal's office to pick up cards and letters that had been sent to me. There were all sorts. The Brookings Institution sent me some of their research on teen pregnancy, which I thought was cool because it showed that they thought I would do more on the topic.

One letter that really surprised me came from the Washington State senate, from Senator Jim Honeyford.

Wow, even the senators are paying attention to what's going on in the little towns, I thought.

I want to congratulate you on your senior project titled "Stereotypes, Rumors, and Statistics." Before making the decision to move forward, a good deal of thought must have gone into this courageous undertaking. Knowing you might be faced with strong criticism from your peers could have been enough to persuade you not to attempt such a feat, but apparently you recognized the value in such a project and willingly played the role of a pregnant teen in order to draw attention to the plight of many teens who in reality find themselves in this difficult situation. . . . In witnessing your supposed unwed pregnant state and the complications surrounding your efforts to continue your education, other students may have seriously contemplated the consequences as well and made some wise decisions which could ultimately lead to fewer teen pregnancies. Again, Gaby, congratulations on your brave move. Your intentions were honorable and I admire your efforts.

Another letter of congratulations came from a woman in New Orleans who had graduated from Toppenish High School in 1943 and wanted to tell me that no one would have been brave enough to do a project like mine back then. Those were the days, of course, where if an unmarried young girl got pregnant, she was hidden away somewhere on "Aunt Edna's farm" until she'd given birth and put the baby up for adoption, and no one in the family would talk about this shameful event again. I'm not sure if it's better or worse that we now put our unmarried young girls on television instead. There has to be a happy medium somewhere between sending a girl into hiding and turning her into a household name.

All the way in New Orleans, this lady found an article about her little hometown, I thought. It was just so strange. People in Toppenish don't make national headlines. It was still hard to believe that I did.

Mr. Cerna called in the school district's public relations

director to help Mr. Greene with the media, but even between the two of them it was just too much. Mr. Greene had a school to run, and he couldn't be consumed with my project full-time; on top of that, no one felt comfortable advising me about the legal consequences or what's standard media practice. He was a school principal; he sure couldn't tell me anything about what I should look for in a film contract or what kind of rights I would give up by sharing my photos with a television network.

The school district's attorney recommended three attorneys I could interview to figure out who I wanted to represent my interests. I went with the one who seemed most grounded and who would take things one step at a time. In turn, she recommended a literary agent for me, and the literary agent recommended a writer for me to work with. Now I had a team. A team! Wasn't that for movie stars?

I also looked to Mr. Greene and Mr. Myers for advice. They told me I should just do one or two national interviews now, and that would put an end to the reporters following me around trying to lock in my first exclusive. It was as if they were getting more and more amped up because I was "hard to get." Mr. Greene and Mr. Myers reminded me that I could have an impact beyond my community by doing this, and I thought about how much it meant to me to get those letters and cards from people inspired by my project.

On my team's advice, we ended up choosing NBC as the

first major network where I'd be interviewed. They seemed to be committed to my future; we wanted to pick a network that would agree to have me back later if I got a book published. I was to fly out to New York with my mom, Saida, Jorge, and Mr. Greene, and go on *The Today Show* and Telemundo.

The only problem was that I was terrified of flying.

Well, not the *only* problem, but the most immediate one. I'd never been on a plane before, and I'd watched one too many scary movies where a plane goes down in flames or breaks apart in midair or gets overtaken by terrorists.

"I don't know if I can come on this trip with you," my mom said. "I have to be here for your grandmother and make sure she gets fed. She's my mother, you know?"

"Mom, you're coming. It's not an option. You're coming to New York with me. Someone else will watch over Grandma."

Among the five of us, she was the only one who'd been on a plane. She'd gone to Texas to see my grandmother's family. I dug my nails into her arm during takeoff and tried not to hyperventilate. I was on a plane to New York City and I was about to meet Matt Lauer and go on television in front of millions of people. *This is not normal.*

Worse, we were on a red-eye flight, so we took off late at night when I should have been sleeping and, of course, I could not fall into a deep sleep. I had to stay awake and prevent the plane from crashing!

I had been warned about turbulence, but the trip was happily uneventful. We got to New York safely and took a car to the hotel. When we got out, we saw a billboard shaped like a baby bottle. It said: OMG. 750,000 TEENAGE GIRLS WILL BECOME PREGNANT THIS YEAR. DON'T BE A STATISTIC.

It was put there by the Candie's Foundation, a nonprofit with the goal of influencing teen culture and changing the way teens think about pregnancy. It was a big ole sign right there in Times Square . . . and it felt like a *sign*. Today was going to be a big day.

CHAPTER 12

GOING BIG

The big day didn't get off to the best start. When we arrived at the hotel, it was too early to check in and our room wasn't ready. All of us were exhausted and wanted to sleep and freshen up from the plane, but the person at the front desk said there was nothing he could do; standard check-in time wasn't until the afternoon. They'd hold our luggage for us, but aside from that, we were adrift in New York City.

I always wanted to see Ground Zero, so that's where we went first. The September 11 tragedy was so unthinkable and had affected everyone in the country, and yet all I really knew of it was from television and newspapers. Going there and seeing the progress being made on the site was inspiring, even though it was also very sad to think about what had happened there. On the day we visited, One World Trade Center had been rebuilt up to the sixty-seventh floor, and steel beams were being put in place for the next floors. It is planned to be the tallest building in the United States.

You couldn't get right up to the site, so we stood near a firehouse, where a man started talking to us about 9/11.

"I worked in the World Trade Center," he said, "but I dropped my son off at school before work. As we were driving, I could see smoke in the distance, and then heard on the radio what had happened."

He told us everything he knew about the plans for the memorial and museum, about what it was like in New York City after the attacks, and about the things he thought the government was covering up. He talked about how the death numbers didn't include the homeless people near the buildings, or the people who were there but not registered to work there. We were transfixed; it was an insider's perspective that we could never have gotten at home in Toppenish.

Once we were allowed to check in to the hotel, my mom went to her room and took a nap while Jorge, Saida, Mr. Greene, and I met with my new agent and lawyer. They said we were pressed for time and should go to a clothing store called H&M for dresses to wear for my big TV appearances. It's a good thing Saida was with me because I had no clue what to even look for. I'm not a dressy person and rarely go shopping, so she helped figure out what would look good on me and acted as my personal stylist.

When we returned, the lawyer and agent brought us into a meeting where they introduced me to my writer, film agent, and a possible publicist. Jorge, Saida, Mr. Greene, and I took the meeting while my mom was still asleep. Here they presented me with a mass of information to consider—Lifetime wanted the film rights, the writer arrived with a tape recorder to start interviews that day, the agent tried to explain book auctions and advances and royalties and subsidiary rights— and my brain was just spinning.

We ate lunch in the conference room while we were talking. Well, mostly *they* were talking and I was listening. One good thing was that they didn't want me to do much media right away, because they wanted to save most of it for after my book and movie came out. *(My book and movie?!)*

Now I understood what people meant by a "whirlwind day." Last month, I had been an anonymous high school student in a small Washington town, and here we were talking about a book and a movie about my life. Did I even want a book and a movie about my life?

"Do I have to make decisions right now?" I asked.

"No," the film agent assured me. "You can think about it, but you can't wait too long. People move on to the next news cycle, so the opportunities that are here for you today may not be here for you in another month or two."

The writer explained that she would do most of her interviews by phone, and Mr. Greene picked up on my hesitancy right away.

"You're worried about using up the minutes on your phone, right?" he asked me.

"Oh! Don't worry—I'll call you," the writer said.

"Still. I don't have a landline. I get charged for incoming calls on my cell phone, too."

It wasn't real to me yet that the money I would make from these deals would more than cover my phone bill. Right now, I was still grounded in the reality that I hadn't yet started my summer job at the fruit warehouse, and where was this extra money going to come from?

Suggestions came from all over the room. "We'll get you a better cell phone plan." "You can talk over Skype for free." "You can do interviews by instant messages." "We'll find you a place to go to use a landline."

But how was I supposed to do these interviews while I was preparing for graduation? "I still have to finish my portfolio and present my findings to the Senior Boards committee," I said.

"You haven't been graded on your project yet?" the agent asked.

"Right," I said. "It's pass or fail."

"Gaby," Mr. Greene said, "I'm going to take a long-shot guess here and say I think you're going to pass."

There was an answer for each of my concerns, but I still felt uncomfortable making major decisions without talking to my mom and without sleeping on it. I didn't have too much time to think, though, because we had to get back to the room and change for my first interview on Telemundo.

An NBC producer arrived to escort us over to the studio in Rockefeller Plaza, where I learned that a beautiful anchorwoman named Carmen Dominicci had flown all the way from Florida just to interview me. She was the picture of perfection, with her shiny hair and long legs, and so warm to us. My fears about doing the interview melted as she made us feel very comfortable.

It was such a long day that I was very happy to finally get under the covers and get some sleep. The following morning we had to leave for the studio at seven a.m., which was four a.m. Pacific time. I was up two hours before that to get ready and have breakfast.

As I sat in the chair getting my hair and makeup done, I felt like I was about to walk the red carpet. The stylists were so good and so fast! I couldn't believe the magic they worked in such a short time. It took me three times as long to do my hair normally, and it didn't come out looking the way they made it look. The makeup women worked on all of us, even the guys.

"I have to wear *makeup?*" Jorge asked. Really, it was just a little foundation and powder to keep the guys' skin from looking shiny under the bright lights for the cameras. But before long, he had found humor in the situation. "Be careful," he said when I came near. "You'll smudge my makeup!"

Before our segment, the camera guys filmed a few shots of me for the quick previews they show of what guest is coming up next. In between those shots, there were lots of people milling around backstage, and when a man came over to talk to me, I initially thought he was another of the many crew members. It took a moment to realize I was looking at Matt Lauer.

"I'm so glad you're here," he said. "How are you doing?"

"I'm well, thanks."

"Do you need anything? Do you want a drink before we go on?"

"No, I'm okay."

I was surprised and happy that he had personally come over to check on us. He smiled and said we'd be on in a few minutes, and reassured me that everything was going to be great. He was shorter than I expected, and easy to talk to.

On camera, he asked me what my peers' initial reaction was when I told them I was pregnant, and whether I felt I had gotten what I wanted out of my project. I told him that I had; even though I knew I couldn't please everybody, I had heard from enough people who were inspired by what I did to know that the project was a success.

Matt commended Jorge for being brave enough to go along with this, and quipped to Mr. Greene that I had set the bar pretty high for next year's senior projects.

"Yeah, how would you like to be a junior doing your project next year?" Mr. Greene joked.

And then it was all over, with Matt wishing us well. It felt really quick; I was surprised they went to all that trouble for the five of us to come to New York just to ask us those few questions. Then the producer sent us on our merry way back into the streets of New York. I didn't want to waste such a great opportunity, so we spent our day sightseeing.

Even though I'm not great with heights, I sucked it up and we went to the Top of the Rock Observation Deck at Rockefeller Center, billed as "New York's most breathtaking view." Jorge went right up to the railing to look out on the city, but I stayed back against the building and said, "Oh, I'm fine right here!" Even from where I stood it was pretty spectacular, but I liked feeling the building right behind me.

After that, we went on a double-decker tour bus all over Manhattan. We wanted to visit the Statue of Liberty, but we had to keep tabs on how much we were spending.

Before we knew it, we were back on a plane to Toppenish, with my agent's words echoing in my mind: "You've bought a winning lotto ticket, and now's the time to cash it in."

Never at any point during this project did I think of it as a way to make money or get famous, and it felt very strange putting it in those terms. This was a very personal subject for me and my family, and if I thought it was hard getting judged and insulted every day in school, how would it be to open myself to the criticism of the world?

But then I thought about my goals for the project. My hope had been to help the students in my school think differently about teen pregnancy. I thought maybe I would be able to reach others in the community. I had never thought beyond that . . . but why not? If I really wanted to make an impact, why not take these opportunities to spread my message on a much larger scale?

The *Yakima Herald-Republic* reporter had been right. This was going to be *big*.

The Today Show aired live while we were in New York, before school hours back in Toppenish. It also appeared online, so Mrs. Straehle and a few other teachers let their students watch the show in class. I didn't get to see it until we were back home, and then my mom, Jorge, and I sat together and watched. We made fun of every little thing—each other's facial expressions and mannerisms, the way Jorge didn't really answer the only question Matt Lauer asked him. (In response to "What were your fears going into this?" Jorge started talking about how his parents didn't speak to him for a week after he told them I was pregnant . . . oops!) We were still on a fun high from the trip—*This really happened. We really went to New York. We were really on the* Today Show. *Can you believe this happened to us?*

The show segment was as short as it felt, which several people at school commented on. They asked me why it was so short, and what Matt Lauer was like, and what New York was like. I think most of them were as surprised as I was that someone from Toppenish had been on national television.

The truth is that I felt a little guilty getting all the attention for my project when my friend Emmanuel should have been sharing that spotlight with me. For his project, he had organized and run a prom just for the special-needs students. It was a terrific project that gave these students a high school experience they normally wouldn't have. That was so worthy of attention, but some of the teachers were concerned about releasing photos and information about it to the newspapers and possibly having the students get teased. I wish that didn't need to be a concern.

The student who had called me a liar kept saying nasty things about me, like that I had done all this for fame. I wondered how that made sense to anyone who saw me running out of the school building in tears, or fleeing the reporters on the school trip. But when I saw him around school, I made sure not to let him see how his comments were affecting me. I smiled and kept my head high, which is the best way I know to deal with people who spread rumors and try to bring others down.

I gave the same advice to the girl in the leadership group; you never want to give bullies the satisfaction of seeing you react emotionally, or it'll continue. If they see you're not affected by their actions, then they'll have no reason to keep it up because they're not winning.

It's so important, instead, to find people who support you and focus on them. You have to be open to support wherever it comes from, and in my case, it often came from nice strangers. After my TV appearances, even more people sent cards and letters to my school. A student named Erin at Grand Valley State University in Michigan wrote:

> I read and saw your story clip on NBC and wanted to congratulate you on your brave doings. I can imagine how hard it must have been for you to have so many people look down on you ... But know that what you did is truly powerful and exhibited the activist in you. As an advocate for comprehensive sex education and support for women, [I want to say] your experiment definitely opened the eyes for many concerning this issue. I hope you continue to strive for social justice and know that your actions are not going unnoticed. Good luck for your future and stay the strong woman that you are.

My church priest wrote to tell me, "Your good mother, your grandmother, your parish family, and I are proud of you."

And people reached out to me on Facebook. Strangers from all over sent me friend requests, and it took me a while to weed through them all. One came from a young man who told me that he related to my background and ambition to succeed. He shared his story with me, and it broke my heart: He came to the United States from Mexico when he was seven years old, by himself, to meet family members who were already here. He worked hard in school and earned a full scholarship to a well-known college in Boston, but just as he was about to start school, the scholarship offer was taken back because the young man didn't have a Social Security number. It was discovered that he was in the country illegally, and he now has a court date to find out if he's being deported. I was amazed by how accepting he seemed of the whole situation; if he has to go back to Mexico, he won't have anything there, and his college dreams will disappear.

It frustrated me to think about all the young people in the United States who don't take advantage of the opportunities given to them so freely, while someone like this man was willing to risk his life at age seven for those same opportunities. He could have been killed trying to cross the border, or arrested, and I can't imagine how scared he must have been.

I can't imagine how scared he must be now. Yet he was writing to me to congratulate me and encourage me to continue with my goals.

The messages from strangers contrasted with the teasing I took from my siblings, who would make comments about how uppity I'd be once I had money.

But I don't have money yet. There's a long contractual process before I actually receive checks for my movie and book deals. By the time you read this, my life may be very different from what is it now, but right now, I'm still working long hours at the fruit warehouse and wearing shoes that are three years old.

The other day hit ninety-three degrees here in Toppenish, and my mother had to drive around in her car that has no air-conditioning, and no tinted windows. The one thing I know I want to do when I have the money is to buy her a new car. I can't stand seeing her suffer like that, and I can't wait to get rid of that stupid car! I'd also like to get myself a car. Beyond that, I don't have any big plans for what to do with the money. It's not enough to buy a mansion or a yacht, but it's enough to make it easier for me to afford what I need during college, which will make it easier for me to concentrate on my studies. That's all I've really wanted from the start.

I still have no desire to be a celebrity. It's kind of funny getting recognized around town, though. When the news first broke, lots of people would ask, "Hey, aren't you the girl who did that senior project?" or "Aren't you the girl who faked her own pregnancy?"

"Yep, that's me," I'd say.

Nowadays, I often see people staring at me in stores, and I can read their minds: *Why do I know that girl? I recognize her. . . . Have I met her before?* Sometimes they still remember where they know me from, and sometimes the memory has faded and they only know they've seen my face *somewhere*.

Even the cashier at 7-Eleven recognized me and asked if I was going to write a book. I told him it was going to be published in a few months, and he asked if I'd please come back to the store when it was out so he could buy a copy and have me autograph it. It's great to have that kind of local support.

People have asked me what it feels like to be a role model for young girls; it feels good. But I'm not unique in that—we're all role models whether we realize it or not. There's always someone watching our behaviors and learning from us, whether that's our little brothers and sisters, nieces and nephews, friends, classmates, neighbors. . . . I've always tried to go through life knowing I'm a role model for my nieces and nephews, long before I did anything to get "famous."

So we're all role models; the only variation is what *kind* of role models we choose to be: good or bad. I'm going to try to be a good one.

Good people are allowed to make mistakes. My mom

wasn't perfect, but she was still a strong role model for me. One of the best things a role model can do is to show how to get through the tough times and live a good life despite setbacks and hardships, because nobody gets through this life without some scars along the way.

To have so much happening for me at such a young age is confusing and great at the same time. My siblings had often told my mom that there should be a book about her life, and in a funny way, now there is. I'm sure I am less judgmental about people because of who my mother is, and her story. Sometimes I think what it takes to make people see that their careless gossip has a ripple effect is to put the face of someone you love to the pain you're causing.

I told the teen moms at my school that they were the ones who inspired me to do my project. It's a very brave thing to choose to give up a baby for adoption, or to keep a baby despite knowing that you don't have your life together yet and you'll now have a big battle ahead. No matter what mistakes they might have made to get themselves in that position, they deserve to have the chance to prove themselves. Some will wind up being doctors, teachers, nurses, business owners, and the mothers of future presidents. Some will learn from their mistakes, devote themselves to parenting, and go on to become great examples for their children. And with enough support, we can tip the odds from "some" to "most."

• • •

I was thinking about this idea—how we are the ones who can change the future—when I stepped into my maroon graduation cap and gown. I had placed in the top 5 percent of my class, and I had been chosen as one of the commencement speakers.

When I gave each of my brothers and sisters their invitations to my graduation ceremony, I laid it on the line for them: "This is the invitation to my graduation, the most important day of my life so far. If you're not here for me on this day, for any reason, I *will* hold it against you for the rest of your life." I probably emphasized that to Genaro most of all.

They kind of chuckled about it, but you know what? They all showed up. So did an aunt and uncle of mine.

Not my dad, though. A few weeks earlier, I tried telling him about my project and my trip to New York and everything else that was happening. He just seemed really unimpressed.

"I haven't seen anything about this," he said.

"You haven't seen it in the newspapers, or on TV, or anything?"

"No."

How could he have missed it? I had strangers stopping me in the mall, but my own father hadn't caught wind of it? I wanted to see him to show him the newspaper clippings and tell him about everything, but he kept putting me off, making excuses. "I don't have gas in my car," he said once.

"Well, why don't we come to you, then?"

"What's the big deal? Why do you keep talking about this project of yours?" he asked.

He told me that his wife didn't want him coming to visit me because she thought he would try to get back together with my mom, and that she also didn't want him going to my graduation.

My mother got on the phone and said, "You can't just see your daughter on your terms. She's tired of this already. She's going away to college and she's making a life of her own. If you don't make any effort to see her now, who knows when you're going to see your daughter again?"

That was four months ago, and I haven't heard a word from him since then.

After eighteen years of trying, it felt like I had done enough. He hadn't been there for my first steps, or my first day of school, or most of my birthdays, or almost any other milestone in my life, and yet I had tried so hard not to give up on him. Now it felt like the time to accept that *he* was the one missing out. I am very lucky to have had a mother with enough love for two parents, and a great boyfriend, friends, and teachers who have believed in me no matter what. It doesn't feel like I'm missing too much, and I've made peace with that.

There are always going to be some people in life who disappoint you and *don't* believe in you like you hoped they would, and you have to find the strength to rise above it and realize that they're wrong. You're still a worthy person whether they think so or not. If there's no one else to tell it to you, then tell it to yourself.

The graduation ceremony was probably like most graduation ceremonies, except that it was *mine*. A flood of memories and feelings washed over me—all the things I'd been through on the path to getting here, and how much my schooling had meant to me. I knew it was the path to a better life, and this was just my beginning. I looked around at the other students, some of whom I remembered from second or third grade, and felt proud of how far all of us had come. Some of the students who used to say, "I can't wait to get out of here," now said, "I can't wait to get out of here . . . to go to college." It was like we had matured as a class.

My whole family got together that day at the high school for a family photo—all eight of us brothers and sisters plus my mom. There hadn't been a photo of all of us together since I was four years old. My mother looked at us and cried. "I never thought I'd be able to get another picture of all of you together," she said. It was a rare moment captured on camera, and it represented something. . . . Through it all, the ups and downs and backwards and sideways, we were still a family.

Standing at the podium before my speech, I looked out at my mother and my grandmother sitting together. Here we were, three generations moving forward together. My grandmother hadn't gone to school at all, my mother had dropped out in the eighth grade, and I would go on to college.

"Fellow graduates, I urge you today to embrace the opportunity before you," I said. "Take what you have learned the last twelve years and put it to good use. Leave behind what isn't helpful and bring forward the significant changes you've made. Be ready to begin the biggest change beyond high school: your life!"

CHAPTER 13

THE FUTURE

As I write this, I'm all packed to go to Columbia Basin College (CBC). I had enrolled there before my project because I liked so much about it—first, it's a fairly small school, and I don't want to get lost in the crowd of a big university. I like the idea of knowing everyone. Second, it's in a bigger city than Toppenish, with more to do and more opportunities, but still close enough that I can come back for frequent visits. And third, they accepted me into their College Assistance Migrant Program (CAMP), which provides not only financial aid but also services like counseling and tutoring for first-year college students. I'll also be in the work-study program, working on campus about nineteen hours a week.

CBC is a two-year college, and after that I'll transfer to either Central Washington University or Eastern Washington

University to complete my bachelor's degree. I'm excited to see what college life is like and to explore my career options.

I plan to go back to my high school for their special events, like the annual talent show and the Mr. Toppenish show, and to keep up with the teachers who have had such a positive impact on my life. I know they're looking forward to seeing what happens next for me, as they had a big role in getting me this far.

My biggest hope going forward is that I can use the platform I've been given to spread the messages of my project. I hope teens will realize that getting pregnant in high school can happen to any girl who is sexually active, and that even the best contraceptives can fail. It's something to take very seriously, because there's nothing acceptable about having a baby before you have your own life together.

I'm not one to judge when anyone is ready to have sex. That's something a couple needs to decide both together and individually, thinking through not just whether or not they feel ready for sex itself, but also the possible consequences. Abstinence is an ideal, but not always a realistic one, so being as safe as possible is the key—using protection every time, no matter what. Stopping yourself before it gets too far to take a breath and take the right precautions.

I know that people usually see sex ed class as a joke, but we need to put more emphasis on understanding the consequences of unprotected sex. My view is that sex ed should be introduced in middle school and expanded on in high school. The parents who opt their kids out of the classes should be prepared to have very honest discussions about it at home.

I also hope that I can get through to the people who think it's acceptable to ostracize pregnant teens and insult them for their mistakes. Their lives are hard enough; they need support, encouragement, and direction if they're going to be able to continue their educations and make a good life for themselves and their children. So if you see a pregnant teen around the halls in school, maybe just take a minute to ask how she's doing and if she needs to talk. A few words of encouragement can go a long way when the messages she's hearing all day are negative.

You don't usually see headlines like PREGNANT TEEN DIDN'T SCREW UP HER ENTIRE LIFE AFTER ALL, but the truth is that there are lots of girls out there who beat the odds. Kymberly Wimberley is a recent example. She was the source of a lot of online attention because, despite being a teen mom, she managed to be her school's valedictorian. After just a few weeks off for her baby's birth, she went right back to school and earned the highest GPA in the graduating class. However, the day after the school's superintendent declared her valedictorian, the principal announced that she was going to have to share the honors—he was appointing a covaledictorian who had a slightly lower GPA.

Why? He said it had to do with the fact that the other girl had half a credit more, even though she had a lower GPA, but Kymberly and her mom believed that the school didn't want a black teen mom as their valedictorian. There was a huge petition online to get her honor reinstated and name her the sole valedictorian again, though as of this writing that hasn't happened.

If she worked her butt off to defy the stereotype, then why would anyone try to take that away from her? Could it be that people don't *want* others to beat stereotypes? Could it be that people who don't fit the mold make it uncomfortable for others to hold on to their prejudices?

Overall, I think that stereotyping is a useless thing that limits people and dooms them to repeat others' mistakes. We are all individuals with our own morals and abilities, and we should have the freedom to make our own paths without people prejudging us based on who our families are, the color of our skin, where we live, or any other outside factors.

It takes hard work to better ourselves and break out of the boxes society wants to put us in. No one should accept a life where they're collecting welfare and scraping by and never really achieving anything for themselves—and I don't say that in a judgmental way. My mother had times when she was on welfare and got medical coupons and food stamps. There are times when government assistance is needed to survive—but that should always be saved for when it's truly necessary, and only for as long as it's truly necessary. No matter what your lot is in life, you can work to educate yourself and find a job that's satisfying and useful *and* pays the bills, so that you can be a good example for the people around you. Because they may need encouragement to do the same thing.

I hope we can change this society so that, instead of teens working hard to tear each other down and laughing about it in the school hallways, we can learn to support each other and help each other move forward when there are troubles along the way.

One day at school, I got called to the principal's office to pick up a bouquet of flowers. It was from a lady who didn't leave any contact information but wrote me a letter. In it, she said that she had gotten pregnant at an early age and her family disowned her. She went through so much, and it was devastating not to have support when she needed it. Then she told me how courageous I was to confront this issue and thanked me for speaking up for people like her.

"You've given a voice I never had to fight against everything that I couldn't," she wrote.

I want to thank everyone who's written to me or about me, congratulating me on my project. It's been very meaningful that my little project has mattered to so many. I hope very much that if you understand and agree with my message, you'll carry it forward, too. I'm not campaigning to be the face of teen pregnancy awareness; I'm just hoping that I've helped to spark thoughts and discussions, and that other people will do things to further the message.

I am just one eighteen-year-old Latina girl from an economically disadvantaged town, raised by a single mom. . . . By society's standards, people don't expect much of me. But I'm going to prove society wrong, and I hope you'll join me.

Our time has come.

ACKNOWLEDGMENTS

From Gaby: Mom, you've fought through so much in your life and you deserve happiness. You're the reason I move forward. You've pushed me to do the best I can, and as I improve my life, I want you right next to me.

Jorge and Saida, you've never hesitated to be there to listen when things have been chaotic, or to laugh with me. You are the best friends I could have, and I appreciate you.

Mr. Myers, thank you for showing me that there's a better world out there, and convincing me that I have the potential to do anything I set my mind to.

To all of my teachers, especially Mrs. Straehle, Mr. Greene, Mrs. Dorr, Ms. Andrews, Mrs. Brulotte, Mrs. Larsen, Mr. Piper, and Mr. Gonzales: Thank you for all your help and inspiration.

Thank you to my project mentors: Mary McCracken, Lori Gibbons, and Julie Valdez. Your time, encouragement, and enthusiasm helped me greatly.

To Nestor, Ismael, Blanca, Cameron, Freddy, Cheese, Manny, Alvaro, and Maria: You've been there for me through the good and bad, and I will always treasure our high school memories.

To my grandmother, brothers, sisters, aunts, uncles,

nieces, and nephews: Even though our lives may take different turns and we don't always agree, no matter what, we're always a family in the end and I love you.

To Zareen Jaffery, Sharlene Martin, and Anne Bremner: Thank you for making the dream of this book a reality.

Thank you also to those who opened up to me about their stories after the project. I wish the best for all of you, and I hope you'll share your stories to inspire others as well.

From Jenna: Gaby, thank you so much for trusting me with this important book; I wish you success in everything you do. Trevor, Juana, Jorge, and Saida, thank you for talking to me and sharing your stories. Zareen Jaffery and the team at Simon & Schuster, thank you for championing this story and believing that it matters. Sharlene Martin, thank you for recommending me to Gaby. To the VIPs in my life—Lisa and Chris Fries, Paul Glatzer, Pat Alch, Keith Potter, Stefanie Smith, Dave Sobel, Susan Markowitz, Scott Rigsby, Samantha Osowski, Kristin Paye Baker, Dan Furst, Frank Baron, and Charlie Stuart—thank you for everything. My sweet Sarina, you are the best daughter a mommy could ever have, and I will always work hard to make you proud.

To the readers, thank you for caring. I love helping people tell their stories, and you're the reason I get to do it.